It's the Busi.....

FOR TRANSITION YEAR

DARINA REGAN AND HILDA O'MALLEY

Gill & Macmillan

Gill & Macmillan Ltd
Goldenbridge
Dublin 8
with associated companies throughout the world
www.gillmacmillan.ie

© Darina Regan and Hilda O'Malley 1999

0 7171 2814 8
Print origination in Ireland by Design Image, Dublin

Contents

Business and You

CHAPTER ONE

Get Working

F ew people who leave school in the twenty-first century will be able to stay in the same job for their entire working life. Frequent job changes and even complete changes in career are becoming the norm. There will be a continual need to update existing skills and acquire new skills to stay one step ahead. The twenty-first century will require **life-long learning**.

Knowledge is power

Your present employment: how do you measure up?

Most of you are already well established in your first career. You clock in for a good day's work, five days a week, with the added bonus of long holidays. It's a relatively secure job, with a very slim chance of being fired! With some luck, you'll find a talent you can work on and develop that could lead to your next career. The pay is determined by each individual worker: the more effort you put in, the greater the return. You could say you are self-employed.

So how do you measure up as a member of the school-going work force?

Go get that job: getting started

All companies, whatever their size, may need to take on extra staff. This could be because

● the business is growing and there is a need for new positions to be filled, or
● because existing posts have become vacant.

It is possible to secure a job by approaching the company first: you can always approach your chosen company in the hope that they might have that dream job. But most people find work by responding to a series of actions initiated by the company.

Just as you are looking for the right job, the business is also looking for the right person. Each stage of the employment process involves activities both for the company looking for employees and for the person looking for a job.

Recruitment is the first stage in filling a vacancy in the business. The recruitment process will involve a careful study of the vacancy, so that the role of the new employee can be clearly defined in a **job description**. The job description sets out

The process of recruitment

Job description
▼
Advertising the post
▼
Application
▼
Screening candidates
▼
Selection
▼
Appointment & induction

Ready!

in broad terms the duties and responsibilities of a particular job. The qualifications required may also be identified: for example, a job description for the post of junior clerk-receptionist for Spice Ltd might include the following information:

Job title:	Junior clerk-receptionist
Job location:	Finance Department
Duties:	Answering the phone
	Office filing (computerised)
	Typing
	Welcoming customers
	General office duties
Reporting to:	Assistant finance manager

Over to you

Who draws up the job description?

Advertising the job

The job may be advertised internally—in a staff magazine or on notice-boards—and may be filled by a member of the existing staff.

Over to you

There are both pros and cons involved when companies hire internally. Draw up a list of the pros and cons.

If there is no suitable internal candidate, there will be a need to advertise the post externally. Various places could be used to advertise the job:

- **newspapers:** local and national;
- **employment agencies:** these help the employer find the right employee by putting them in contact with suitable candidates on their files. If the agency fills a vacancy, the employer pays a fee;
- **word of mouth:** informing friends and acquaintances of the vacancy;
- **the internet:** a new and effective means of advertising vacancies.

Over to you

1 Name the newspapers that carry recruitment sections. Do they appear every day?

2 Scan the newspapers to find examples of advertisements for jobs.

3 You work in the Personnel Department of Spice Ltd. Where would you advertise the post of junior clerk, and why?

A typical job advertisement

Spice Ltd

A leading food manufacturer requires a junior clerk-receptionist at its offices in Killarney.

Applicants, ideally school-leavers, should have a (minimum) of
three Leaving Certificate subjects, including Mathematics and
English, and an outgoing personality and should be able to
communicate with customers, both on the phone and in
person.

This is an interesting and varied job, requiring enthusiasm
and commitment.

The salary will be in the range (£8,500–9,500) with twenty-five
days' holiday a year. A (subsidised canteen) is available.

*The closing date for receipt of (completed application forms) is 8
December 1999. For an application form and further details write to:*

Ms Geraldine Halliway

Personnel Department

Spice Ltd

Muckross Road

Killarney

Co. Kerry

Over to you

Having read this advertisement, answer the following questions.

1 Are three Leaving Cert subjects absolutely necessary to secure the job? Mary
got six As in her Leaving Cert; does this mean she is doubly qualified for the
post and has the job in the bag? Consider the case of Johnny (Mary's twin),
who has two Leaving Cert subjects and experience of working as a
receptionist. Should Johnny bother applying for the job?

2 Why does the salary vary between £8,500 and £9,500?

3 You are on a economy drive; you have a choice of eating in the staff canteen
or the local coffee shop. Which would you choose, and why?

4 Mary wants to write about her talents, qualifications, and hobbies, and the
application form simply does not give enough space. Can she send a CV
instead?

Steady ...

A well-designed application form serves to screen or eliminate obviously unsuitable applicants.

Interested people will now send for further details and an application form. The Personnel Department will send out a standard printed form, which helps to give a precise picture of the person applying for the job and the candidate's suitability.

A typical job application form

● Spice Ltd ●

Application for the post of _____

Full name: _____

Full address: _____

_____

_____

Telephone number: _____

Date of birth: ☐ ☐ ☐

Education (secondary): name and address of school attended, starting and finishing dates:

Qualifications: examinations and grades, dates: _____

_____

Work experience: starting and finishing dates: _____

_____

Positions of responsibility held: _____

_____

Part-time activities, hobbies, and interests: _____

Name and address of two referees: _____

_____

I certify that to the best of my knowledge the information given above is correct.

Signature: _____   Date: _____

Over to you

You are applying for the job of junior clerk-receptionist. Fill out the application form printed above.

Reality check for applicants

Keep in mind that the application form is the first impression the company will obtain of the applicant, and it will be used in comparing applicants. It will later be used to select certain candidates for interview.

As it is the first stage in the selection process, it is important that you complete the form clearly and carefully. First impressions last!

Providing a CV

The advertisement requested those interested in the job to send for an application form and further details. Instead, the company could have asked the applicant to send a *curriculum vitae (CV)*. The CV should contain brief, relevant information on the applicant; the following headings should act as a guideline.

CURRICULUM VITAE

Name: _____

Home address: _____

Date of birth: _____

Place of birth:_____

Nationality: _____

Education (second and third level): _____

Qualifications:_____

Interests and activities: _____

Work experience:_____

Referees: _____

Over to you

Now prepare your own CV. Keep it informative, but concise.

The CV is usually accompanied by a *covering letter*—a short letter explaining why you think you are suitable for the job and requesting an interview. Don't underestimate the importance of that covering letter: it is often the key to getting to the next stage—the interview.

Careful assessment of the application forms or CVs will result in the company choosing the suitable candidates for interview. A *short-list* of the applicants best suited to the job will then be drawn up. The employer must then assess which candidates are most suitable for the job advertised.

The *interview* is one of the most commonly used methods of selection. It allows the company to make a judgment on

—the candidate's personality;

—the ability of the candidate to communicate;

—whether the information on the application form or CV is accurate.

It gives the candidate the chance to find out more about the business, such as the working conditions, hours of work, pay, and training. This is an opportunity for the candidate to shine or fade.

Other methods of selection include:

- **aptitude tests:** these can cover areas such as mental abilities, for example powers of reasoning;
- **physical tests:** these are essential for certain jobs: for example, potential pilots and gardaí have eyesight tests;
- **group discussion or observation:** this method is sometimes suitable when the company is selecting from a large number of applicants.

Medical tests may also be necessary before the job offer is confirmed. This will give a clear indication whether the candidate is physically suitable for the work.

While these selection tests do not provide a guarantee of how the candidate will perform once employed, they can draw attention to the candidate's ability to do the job.

Go!

The contract of employment

Having selected the person who appears to be most suited for the post, the employer will formally offer the job, usually in writing. Once the candidate has accepted the post, a letter and contract of employment are sent confirming the appointment.

Induction

Many companies recognise the anxiety involved in starting a new job. To make the transition into the new role as painless as possible, companies may organise *induction courses*. The new employee needs to be introduced to the new working environment in much the same way that first-year pupils are shown the ropes at the beginning of term, so that they can become familiar with their new surroundings.

Induction provides

—instructions about the job;

—information about health and safety regulations, payment details, etc.;

—information about the values, beliefs or code of ethics of the company.

The new employee may also have a **probation period** to work through before being offered a permanent position.

A job for life—fact or fiction?

At the outset, it was pointed out that few people have the security of a job for life. The 'normal' working life will involve breaks in your career—whether you've planned for them or not. This can happen in the following ways:

1 Redundancy: this occurs when the company doesn't have enough work for the people presently employed. It may happen in the following ways:

- *natural wastage:* this arises when people retire or leave to take up a better job; when they leave, the vacancy is not filled;
- *voluntary redundancy:* the business wants to reduce the work force and entices workers to volunteer to leave by offering a cash incentive; this could be a positive thing, as it may 'push' you to make the leap into self-employment;
- *compulsory redundancy:* in certain cases the business may reduce the work force in order to survive, and so workers lose their jobs.

Over to you

Can you name any companies that have offered redundancy packages in recent times?

2 Retirement: in Ireland, men and women retire at the age of sixty-five. The employee may have paid in to the company's pension scheme, and this will mean that they will obtain a pension on retirement based on the number of years of service.

Over to you

There are many people over sixty-five who are still working. How can this be so if retirement is the 'norm' at that age?

3 Dismissal: this means being sacked from a job because of incompetence, dishonesty, or breach of the company's rules.

4 Career break: people take career breaks for several reasons, including

—to pursue further study (in preparation for a career change);

—to pursue a cause;

—to set up a business;

—for family reasons.

5 End of contract.

It is becoming the norm to be employed on a contract basis: once the particular project is completed the contract of employment is ended.

Actively seeking a job

Finding yourself without employment while actively looking for a job can be a traumatic event. Securing that next job is not easy! But all is not lost. There are several possible options, including

● further education;

● exploring the possibility of setting up a new business;

● using your talents or hobbies as a springboard to new opportunities.

Some guidelines to keep in mind

1 You will have to organise your time. A job organises a worker's time; if you are unemployed, the task of organising your time is left to yourself.

2 Unemployment means out of a **job** but not out of **work**.

Over to you

List the **work** you might be able to do if you were unemployed

—for your family;

—for your community;

—for yourself.

3 Short-term pain for long-term gain: offering your skills free of charge can help to keep you busy while adding to your skills. Multi-skilling—training yourself in a variety of jobs—may set you apart.

4 Nobody will come to tell you about financial entitlements, so find out now. Research has shown that many people do not receive what they are entitled to, mainly through lack of knowledge.

Over to you

Identify the sources of such information.

5 Working abroad for a short or a long period may also be a possibility. It may provide an opportunity for expanding your work (and life!) experiences.

6 Self-employment should also be considered. Create your own job rather than waiting for someone to offer you one. Be your own boss!

Over to you

Richard Branson, Feargal Quinn and Margaret Heffernan all have something in common. What is it?

Besides being wealthy, each of them is their own boss. They are self-employed.

Go to
You in Business

Join the Team. Enjoy the Rewards.

To find out more come to our

OPEN DAYS

TUESDAY 25TH AUGUST
Great Southern Hotel, Eyre Square Galway

WEDNESDAY 26TH AUGUST
Limerick Ryan Hotel, Limerick

THURSDAY 27TH AUGUST
Royal Dublin Hotel, Dublin
and
Royal Marine Hotel, Dun Laoghaire

THURSDAY 27TH AUGUST
Temple Gate Hotel, Ennis

FRIDAY 28TH AUGUST
Imperial Hotel, Cork

If you get on well with people, you'll get on well at Dunnes Stores.
Whether you're male, female, young or young at heart, starting fresh into the workplace or returning to employment - we want you to join our team.

- Flexible hours to suit **Part Time Sales Assistants**. (15 - 30 hours per week)
- Highly competitive rates of pay.
- Training is given to enable all employees to deliver the highest standard of customer service.
- Generous Pension Plan and VHI Scheme available.
- PLUS there are opportunities for promotion and personal development.

DUNNES STORES
The difference is... We're Irish

Now that you've got brilliant results, it's time you got a brilliant career.

If you are one of the clever students who got at least three A's in your Leaving Certificate results earlier this week, Ark Life would like to talk to you about a really clever career move. We have excellent opportunities in our Actuarial Department for Trainee Actuaries who are interested in a career with a uniquely successful Life Assurance company.

TRAINEE ACTUARIES

Our Actuarial Team are key drivers of our business, through their work on designing quality products and managing the financial aspects of the business.

We are expanding the team to support a number of significant business initiatives and we are looking for high calibre trainees. Leaving Cert students must have a minimum of 3 A's on higher level papers, including Maths. We are also interested in applications from graduates who have achieved at least a 2.1 honours degree in Maths or maths-related subjects.

We will provide comprehensive support with further study, excellent opportunities to gain a wide variety of work experience, and an attractive remuneration package.

If you would like to be considered for one of these positions, please send a copy of your results and curriculum vitae in strict confidence to:

Mr. Brendan J. Breen,
Human Resources & Training Manager,
Ark Life Assurance Company Limited,
8 Burlington Road, Dublin 4.

Completed applications must be received by Monday, 31st August 1998.

Ark Life is an equal opportunities employer.

Ark Life

AIB's Life & Pensions Company

Assignment

Read the advertisements above, which appeared in the recruitment section of a national newspaper, then answer the following questions:

1 Who are these job advertisements aimed at?

2 In which of the jobs is experience required or essential?

3 Give *two* benefits—apart from salary—that successful applicants might receive.

4 What other information would you want to have before applying for any of the jobs?

5 How do you apply for these jobs?

6 Which job would *you* apply for, and why?

CHAPTER TWO

Working Together

Now that you have a job, remember that you have certain responsibilities.

- Be on time for work.
- Be honest, and do a good day's work.
- Respect your employer's property.

If the shoe is on the other foot and you become an employer, remember that you have certain responsibilities to employees.

- Pay them a fair wage.
- Make sure they have safe and healthy working conditions.
- Obey the laws relating to employment: holidays, unfair dismissal, etc.
- Keep records for income tax and PRSI purposes.

Trade unions

As a new employee, you may be asked by the other workers to join a trade union to which all the others belong. Here's what a trade union will do for you:

1. It protects your interests by negotiating with the employer for better wages, holidays, and working conditions.
2. Union representations are made at national level with the Government and other 'social partners'.

Members of a union subscribe to its funds by means of a **subscription**, or **union dues**, which may be deducted from their wages as they are paid.

Over to you
Is union membership compulsory or voluntary?

Examples of trade unions
Irish Nurses' Organisation (INO)
Services, Industrial, Professional and Technical Union (SIPTU)
Civil and Public Service Union (CPSU)
Irish Bank Officials' Association (IBOA)

Over to you
Can you think of any others?

The unions' umbrella organisation

Most trade unions are members of the Irish Congress of Trade Unions (ICTU), which represents the interests of the trade union group as a whole.

Over to you

Can you name some unions under the ICTU umbrella?

Industrial relations

The relationship between employers and employees is like any other relationship: it can run smoothly, when both are achieving their goals, or it can hit a rough patch.

Hitting the rough patch

This is where problems can arise because of conflict in the relationship:

- Workers may want better wages; the employers say they cannot afford it.
- The employees may want longer holidays but the employers feel that the holidays are adequate.
- The employers would like the workers to be more productive, but the employees feel they are producing to their capacity.

Over to you

Can you think of other causes of conflict that can arise?

When conflict arises, this can often lead to a dispute, which can result in a strike. It is important for both sides to try to resolve their differences as soon as possible. How?

1. The trade union's representative—the *shop steward*—can meet the employer and try to solve the problem. The shop steward is a member of the union elected by the other members to represent them in their work-place.
2. If this fails, other options are available to them. They can decide to appoint a third party to listen to both sides of the dispute and suggest a solution.
3. If they are still in dispute, they can seek help under the Industrial Relations Act (1990) through the Labour Relations Commission (LRC). The commission offers several services to help solve the dispute, including *conciliation*, where the decisions are not binding.

Industrial problems can sometimes result in a strike. Strikes cost both parties money: the employee is not working and so does not get paid; the employer may lose sales if orders are not met. So it is in the interest of both sides to keep industrial

Strikes cost money

unrest to a minimum. This can be done by making sure that clear channels of communication are open at all times.

Conflict management

In recent times, industrial unrest has been significantly reduced by means of **collective bargaining** at national level. The latest agreement is called 'Partnership 2000' and is an agreement regarding pay and working conditions negotiated by the 'social partners'—the Government, employers, farming organisations, and the trade unions.

The Irish Business and Employers' Confederation (IBEC) represented the employers at these negotiations.

Over to you

Who represented the trade unions? Why do these parties agree to come together? What has each party to gain?

Did you know that you too have protection as a young person if you are working?

Protection of Young Persons (Employment) Act (1996)

1. If you are under eighteen, you may not be employed for more than forty hours a week, or eight hours a day.
2. The maximum working week for fifteen-year-olds is
   —8 hours in term time
   —35 hours for holiday work
   —40 hours during work experience.
3. If you are under sixteen, an employer must
   —see a copy of your birth certificate
   —get the written permission of your parents or guardian.
4. The act also contains rules on early morning and night work and on rest periods.

Over to you

1 Why do you think the Dáil passed this legislation?

2 Do you agree or disagree with this law?

3 If you could change this law, what changes would you make?

4 Should people under the age of fifteen be allowed to work as many hours as they wish?

Assignment

The following article appeared in the journal *Business News*:

Possible redundancies at Jingle Bells

Jingle Bells Ltd has announced that there is a possibility that they will have to reduce their work force in the near future. "We are facing increased competition, particularly from low-cost foreign producers, and we need to become more cost-effective if we are to survive," said the managing director, Nicholas Christie.

Having read the article, Peig Sheehan, the shop steward at Jingle Bells Ltd, said: 'We know nothing of these changes. We'll have to hold a meeting of our members and subsequently meet the management. Redundancies are not on.'

When Nicholas Christie read the article he said: 'Typical journalists: they blow things out of all proportion. I made a mistake: I should have spoken to the union first to prevent crossed wires.'

1 Before the meeting organised by the shop steward, many of the workers were calling for an immediate strike. Why might they want to go for this option first?

2 Other workers thought that other methods of solving the problem should be tried before going on strike. What might these methods be, and why would the union consider them?

A meeting took place, and the following statement was issued: 'The management of this company is considering purchasing new machinery for the factory. This may lead to a reduction in staffing levels. Full consultation with the union will take place at all stages, and there will be no compulsory redundancies.'

3 Why do changes at work often worry the people involved?

4 What do the management mean by 'full consultation with the union will take place at all stages'? What do you think will be the main points of their discussions?

Project work

Are you aware of any labour disputes in recent times? You may even have seen a *picket line* in operation. Scan the news—in the papers, on television or radio—and answer the following questions:

1 Why did the dispute start?

2 What sort of action is being taken?

3 Is this dispute official or unofficial?

4 Is the work-place being picketed?

5 How would you resolve the dispute?

6 Follow the dispute until it is resolved. How was it resolved?

CHAPTER THREE

Account for Life

The main financial institutions operating in Ireland today include:

- commercial banks
- state banks—for example ACC, ICC
- the Trustee Saving Bank (TSB)
- building societies
- An Post
- credit unions.

Over to you

Some of these are broad categories of financial institutions.

1 Name the commercial banks.

2 Name three building societies.

3 In your opinion, why do people choose one financial institution instead of another?

As most people will at some stage in their life operate a bank account, the services provided by commercial banks will be the main focus of this chapter.

Businesses are set up to provide a product or a service; just as supermarkets sell groceries, financial institutions sell a range of accounts and other financial services. The two most commonly used accounts are **deposit accounts** and **current accounts**.

Deposit account or current account—that is the question

These are the main types of account available to us as consumers of banking services. Which you choose depends on your needs.

Deposit account

- This type of account is used for investing money safely.
- You earn interest.
- You can withdraw your money using withdrawal slips or an ATM.
- Deposit accounts come in many forms: the banks 'segment' the customers, using age as one of the criteria.

More later

Current account

The main difference between a deposit account and a current account is that the current account usually earns no interest. You can withdraw your money using several methods, principally by means of cheques but also by using cash machines (ATMs) and withdrawal slips.

The catch!

With the bank's permission, you may be able to take money out of your account even though it's empty. This is called an **overdraft**. You will have to pay high interest for this service.

If you wish to open either of these accounts you will have to visit the bank and fill in an application form.

Over to you

What information will they be looking for?

Application form for a bank account

Mark O'Brien, 10 Rochestown Drive, Cork, visited the local bank last week to open a current account, and he lodged £200 to this account at the time.

Help Mark to complete the application form opposite.

Lodging money in a bank account

Today Mark wishes to lodge £75.88 in cash and a cheque for £50 that he received from his aunt into his account.

Help Mark fill in the lodgment slip below.

LODGMENT RECORD SUBJECT TO VERIFICATION	**LODGMENT**	**Bank of Ireland**

Name(s)

Account Number

£

Please specify Account:
Current ☐ **Savings** ☐
Other ☐

Note: Cheques, etc., are accepted subject to examination and verification and are transmitted for collection.
Though credited to account when paid in they should not be drawn against until cleared. Customers should keep details of cheques lodged.

Thank you for banking with us.

963487

4-92 (R1096) IDFA JN7

Please specify Account: **Current** ☐ **Savings** ☐ **Other** ☐

Name(s)

Address

Date

Paid in by

Brand/Initials

SERIAL NUMBER

FOR BANK USE

Customer's Account Number

Tx

Notes	
Coin	
Total Cash	
Cheque Total	
Total £	

⑆963487⑆

60

| Bank Use Only | 1. New Account No. | | | | | | | | | | 2. New Account No. |

☞ Please note that the details you are being asked to supply may be used to provide you with information, by way of direct marketing, about other products and services supplied by the Bank of Ireland Group, or arranged by the Bank of Ireland Group with third parties.

In holding this information on data file, Bank of Ireland will at all times honour its duty of confidentiality and its responsibilities under the Data Protection Act.

If you do not wish to receive direct marketing offers on the basis of the information supplied above, please tick the box opposite.

CONFIDENTIAL

Customer details *(please use block capitals)*	Applicant (1)	Applicant (2)
	Surname (Mr / Mrs / Ms / Other)	Surname (Mr / Mrs / Ms / Other)
	First Names	First Names
	Address	Address
	Telephone (home)	Telephone (home)
	Date of Birth	Date of Birth
	Marital Status	Marital Status
	Married ☐ Single ☐ Widowed ☐ Other ☐	Married ☐ Single ☐ Widowed ☐ Other ☐
	Dependent Children Number ☐ Aged ☐ to ☐	Dependent Children Number ☐ Aged ☐ to ☐
	Occupation	Occupation
	Employers Name and Address	Employers Name and Address
	Telephone (work)	Telephone (work)
	Net Monthly Income £	Net Monthly Income £
	Estimated Disposable Income £	Estimated Disposable Income £
	Are you paid Monthly ☐ Fortnightly ☐ Weekly ☐	Are you paid Monthly ☐ Fortnightly ☐ Weekly ☐
	Will your income be paid directly to your Account ? (Y/N)	Will your income be paid directly to your Account ? (Y/N)
	Is your position pensionable ? (Y/N)	Is your position pensionable ? (Y/N)

(either applicant to complete)

	Applicant (1)	Applicant (2)
	Residential Status	Do you have credit cards ? (Y/N)
	Owner ☐ With Parents ☐ Tenant ☐ Other ☐	Access ☐ Visa ☐ Other (specify)
	Years at present address	With which bank is your credit card ?
	If a home owner please complete	Bank of Ireland ☐ Other (specify)
	Value of Home £	
	Name of mortgage company	
	Mortgage outstanding £	Do you have Life Assurance ? (Y/N)
	Mortgage type Repayment ☐ Endowment ☐	Name of assurance company
	Year Mortgage taken out	Monthly premium £

SAVINGS	Amount	Company
Bank		
Building Society		
Other		

BORROWINGS	Amount	Company
Bank		
Finance Co.		
Other		

Ref: 4-308

Bank of Ireland ⬢

Taking money out of an account—making a withdrawal

To withdraw money from an account you have several options:

- use a withdrawal slip
- use the ATM (cash machine)
- write a cheque (current account only)
- use a debit card (e.g. 'Laser').

Over to you

Shortly after leaving the bank, Mark spotted a deluxe puncture repair kit for his bicycle. He needed £10 to buy it, and so needed to get his hands on some of the money he had just lodged. He returned to the bank to fill in the following withdrawal slip. Give him a hand.

WITHDRAWAL RECORD	WITHDRAWAL	Bank of Ireland
Name(s)	Please specify Account: **Current** ☐ **Savings** ☐ **Other** ☐	
Account Number	Received the sum of (words) _____ Date:	**JOINT SAVINGS ACCOUNT** I certify that all parties in the Account are alive at this date. Signed:
£	Name of Account Holder(s)	
Please specify Account: **Current** ☐ **Savings** ☐ **Other** ☐ _____	Signature(s)	
	Brand/Initials	SERIAL NUMBER □□□□□ Address
	Customer's Account Number □□□□□□□ Tx	£
Thank you for banking with us		

Problem page

Dear Aunt Aggie,
I've just started a new job and I've opened a current account. The bank gave me a plastic card and a chequebook. I'm a little confused about how to use them.
Mark O'Brien,
Cork.

Here's Aunt Aggie's advice:

1   The cash machine or ATM

To use an ATM ('automated teller machine') you need an ATM card and a personal identification number (PIN). Today the card is both a cheque guarantee card and an ATM card. It has a magnetic strip on the back that stores information about your account. The PIN is a code you must enter each time you use the ATM. You can use the machine to

—take money out of your account

—transfer money between accounts

—pay certain bills, such as the ESB and Telecom Éireann

—lodge money to your account

—check your balance on the screen

—request a bank statement

—order a chequebook.

2 Cheques

This sample cheque should help you when writing your own:

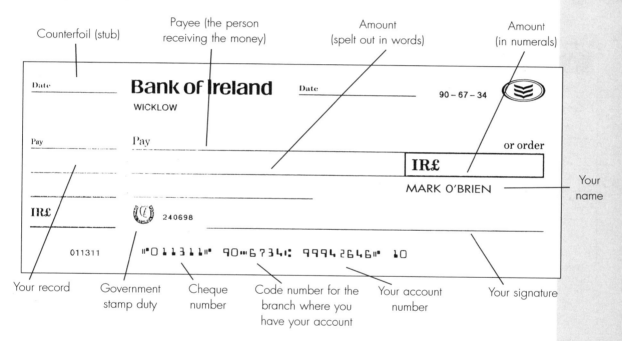

When you are writing a cheque, it is important to fill it in completely and accurately. If it is not filled in properly it can lead to problems. Don't forget to fill in the stub: it's your record.

3 Cheque guarantee card

The bank guarantees to honour the cheque, that is, to pay the amount to the payee, up to a certain limit (this amount is printed on your card). It is more than likely that you received an all-in-one card, combining cheque guarantee card and ATM card. The signature on the back of the card must match the signature on cheques you sign; so be consistent when signing cheques.

Using banking services to pay bills

If you wish to pay your bills using the bank network, you have several options:

1 ATM

2 Credit transfer (also called bank giro)

You can use this service if you wish to lodge money to somebody else's account. You take the money into the bank and fill in the following form (the form varies, depending on the bank):

Bank and branch where money is going

Code of branch where money is going

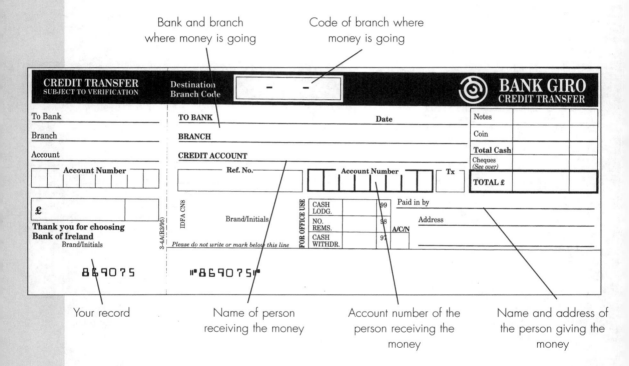

Your record

Name of person receiving the money

Account number of the person receiving the money

Name and address of the person giving the money

3 Standing order (SO)

You arrange with the bank to pay a **fixed** amount at regular intervals out of your account into another account: for example, Mark pays rent of £200 a month out of his account and into the landlady's account.

4 Direct debit (DD)

Certain bills—such as ESB and phone bills—arrive at regular intervals but the amount owed varies, so a standing order is not very useful. Instead you can avail of direct debit, whereby you allow the bank to take money out of your account when it is contacted by certain service providers, such as the ESB and Telecom Éireann.

5 Bank draft

If you wish to pay a bill by cheque but haven't got a current account, you can buy a cheque drawn on the bank, called a bank draft.

Over to you

Mark's mother wants to send him £30, but she has a slight problem: she hasn't got a current account but wants to send a cheque. She has decided to buy a bank draft. Help her fill in the application form.

Your record

Payee (the person who is to receive the money)

DRAFT/GIFT CHEQUE RECORD	APPLICATION FOR DRAFT/GIFT CHEQUE	Bank of Ireland

Draft No.		In favour of			FOR BANK USE ONLY CLEARED VALUE ☐
In favour of			Draft ☐		Signed:
			Gift Cheque ☐		
		Applicant	Date		**Commission**
Applicant		Address			Total Cash
£			Draft No.		Cheques
Brand/Initials		Brand/Initials	Account Number	Tx	Total £
			9 9 9 4 0 3 3 3	60	

Thank you for choosing
Bank of Ireland

3-5 (R8/91)

Name and address of the person buying the draft

6 Debit card—the card of the future

This card allows you to pay for goods without having to use cheques or cash.

How does it work? You give your debit card—like an ATM card—to the cashier where you are making the purchase, who passes it through a card-reader. The cashier enters the amount in the machine. The transaction is automatically checked and authorised, and the money is transferred from your account to the shop's account. A receipt is issued, which you sign. The debit card available today operates under the brand name 'Laser'.

7 Paypath

This is used by employers to pay employees. Your wages are lodged directly into your account from your employer's account.

Understanding your bank statement

From time to time Mark will receive bank statements, which are simply records of all payments into and out of his account over a certain period.

Bank charges

We have seen that the banks and other financial institutions provide a wide range of services. Can you name them?

Over to you

As with any service, you must pay for bank services, and these *bank charges* appear in your bank statement. The charges can be broken down as follows:

- account maintenance fee
- self-service transaction charges—for example using an ATM, direct debit, standing orders, 24-hour banking
- paper or staff-assisted transactions—for example cheques; withdrawals or lodgments at a branch
- Government duty: this is a tax that is paid on cheques and some bank cards; it does not go to the bank but to the Government.

It is interesting to note that almost half the banks' personal customers do not pay current account charges. Investigate why this is so.

Remember

- The more services you use, the more charges you pay.
- Shop around for the best deal.
- A code of practice has been agreed with the Director of Consumer Affairs; leaflets giving details of the principal bank charges are available in branches of the main banks.

Bank of Ireland

CURRENT A(OUNT

Post to		90-07-62
		Branch Code
Michael Lynch,		70
13 Woodlands Park,		Statement Number
Palmerstown,		30 MAR 1992
Dublin 20		Date of Statement
		74107628
		Account Number

Date	Details	Debit	Cdit	Balance
1992				
28 FEB	BALANCE FORWARD			1,081
8 MAR	CHEQUE 393	126		955
10 MAR	CHEQUE 392	54		901
11 MAR	CREDIT TRANSFER		100	1,001
13 MAR	ATM	150		851
20 MAR	FIRST N.B.S. SO	160		691
22 MAR	IRISH LIFE DD	68		623
27 MAR	CHEQUE 395	120		503
29 MAR	CURRENT ACC. Fees	6		497

Thank you for banking with us

Assignment

1 Who received this bank statement, and what is their account number?

2 Was there money in this account on 28 February or was there an overdraft?

3 What happened on 11 March?

4 Where is cheque number 394?

5 Why are the cheque numbers not in sequence?

6 On 29 March, current account fees appear on the statement. Can you give some examples of what these fees might be?

7 What other bank services has the account-holder used?

'Techno-banking': toward a cashless society

1 Multi-card ('plastic banking')
This is an ATM card, cheque guarantee card and debit card all in one.

2 'Smart card'—the electronic purse
This is used for small purchases: it is expected to be used to pay for public transport, parking meters, etc It is like an electronic purse, charged up with electronic value. When the value runs out, the card can be recharged at an ATM with value from the card-holder's account. This system is being piloted at present in Ennis, County Clare, as part of the 'technology town' scheme.

3 24-hour banking—'telebanking'
Telephone banking means that banking services are available day and night, at weekends, and during holidays. It is safe, as personalised numeric codes (like a PIN) are used as a security measure. It is expected that voice recognition will be used in the future.

4 Banking over the internet—the virtual bank
Most of the bigger financial institutions have internet sites, which give information about their services and allow you to bank using the worldwide web (WWW).

5 Other developments
Other developments include
—**'bank shops'**: basic financial services provided in the foyer of a shopping centre, for example Bloomfield's Shopping Centre in Dún Laoghaire;
—**satellite banking**: temporary banking, providing skeleton services during special events;
—**drive-through banking**: availing of banking services from the comfort and safety of a car e.g. AIB, Correlscourt, Dublin.

Customer satisfaction

Consumers of banking services sometimes have cause for complaint; so here is some help with what to do:

1 Explain your problem to the branch of the bank involved.
2 If this does not resolve the issue, contact the customer relations department at the bank's head office.
3 If you still haven't received satisfaction you can contact the Ombudsman for Credit Institutions. This office was set up in 1993 by the banking industry and in 1997 dealt with over a thousand complaints—so you're not alone!

Assignment

1 Distinguish between a deposit account and a current account.

2 What is an overdraft?

3 Is an overdraft facility free?

4 How can you withdraw money from

(a) a deposit account and

(b) a current account?

5 Why might a bank refuse to cash a cheque?

6 What is the cash limit on a cheque guarantee card?

7 Why is it important to keep the cheque stub after writing a cheque?

8 What do the following initials stand for?

ATM

PIN

CT

SO

DD

OD.

9 What are the advantages of Paypath

(a) to the employer and

(b) to the employee?

10 Explain the difference between a laser card and an ATM card.

CHAPTER FOUR

Building the Nest-Egg

To spend or to save?

These are your options when you are deciding what to do with your money. Saving means not spending your money—saving for a holiday, for a car, for new clothes, or that rainy day. You can save your money in a piggy-bank, but it is lying idle when it could be working for you to earn more money.

The wise consumer

If you decide to invest your money (hopefully to make more money!), it pays to shop around and see which form of investment is the best for you.

What should you consider before investing your money?

1 The rate of return

This means how much your money will earn for you. It is sometimes referred to as the growth rate or the rate of interest.

Example: If I invest £50 for one year and at the end of the year my return is 70p, then my rate of return is

$$\frac{70}{5,000} \times \frac{100}{1} = 1.4\%$$

2 Safety

Will my £50 be safe? Is there a chance that I could lose some or all of my money? If the risk is high, then I expect a higher rate of return as a reward. This extra reward is the reason people are sometimes prepared to invest their hard-earned cash in high-risk projects, for example oil exploration.

3 Liquidity

How quickly can I get access to my £50 if I need it—for example, if the rainy day arrives sooner than expected?

4 Tax

Over to you

Will I have to pay tax if I make a good return (profit) on my investment? Can you name any such taxes?

5 Inflation

Will £50 today buy the same amount of goods as £50 did in 1970? The answer is clearly no. This is because of *inflation*—a fall in the value of money, or a rise in general prices.

When examining your options, don't forget:

- safety
- access
- return.

Problem page

Dear Aunt Aggie,

I've just won £15,000 in the lottery, and I'm writing to ask you for some advice on how I should invest my fortune.

Mary Prendergast,

Dublin.

Here's Aunt Aggie's advice:

Congratulations, Mary! Not only have you won £15,000 but it is also tax-free. Where to invest your money depends on

—**safety:** the risk of losing your £15,000;

—**access:** if you need the money, whether you can get it back in a hurry; and, of course,

—**the return:** how much it will earn, and where it will earn the most.

You also need to consider whether you wish to invest your money for a short or a long time. Essentially you have four options:

1. Invest your money in a deposit account in a financial institution. They have several options available. Obviously the longer-term options will earn you more interest. These options are only a phone call away.

2. **Shares:** When you buy a share you become a part-owner of a company. When buying shares in publicly quoted companies you can hope to gain in two ways:

    (a) you receive a part of the company's profit—this is called a *dividend*;

    (b) if the share price increases you can sell it and so make a profit.

You run the risk that the company may make no profit and that the share price may fall.

3. **Bonds:** One of the ways in which the Government earns money is by selling bonds. Bonds represent a source of finance for the Government. The Government borrows money from you and pays you for the use of your money. Your investment is guaranteed, and you will receive a fixed rate of return. Like shares, bonds can be bought and sold on the Stock Exchange—the share market. Government bonds are also known as 'gilts'.

4. **Property:** Money can also be invested in 'bricks and mortar'. Gains can be made in two ways:
   1. You get income from renting the property.
   2. If the value of the property increases, it can be sold at the higher price.

Having decided whether you wish to invest for the short term or the longer term, you should examine what kind of return you want and how much risk you are prepared to accept.

Shares offer a very good return in the long term, but there is no guarantee that share prices will increase.

To hedge your bets, you may decide to invest some money in a deposit account, some in shares, and the rest in bonds, thus creating an 'investment portfolio'. The decision ultimately rests with you.

Aunt Aggie

Other investment alternatives

1 Life assurance

Some life assurance policies combine protection and investment, for example an *endowment policy*. Having paid your premiums, you will receive a lump sum at an agreed future time or on death (if it happens first).

2 Investing in a business

This can involve

—setting up your own business;

—becoming a 'sleeping partner' (it's not what you might think!)—investing your money but not taking an active role.

All may not be as it appears!

1 DIRT

The interest you receive on a deposit account is taxed. This tax is known as *deposit interest retention tax* (DIRT). The interest you receive is your net interest, that is, the interest earned after tax.

2 Capital gains tax

You may think that investing in shares and making a killing when prices are rising rapidly is a great way to go, but if you sell your shares and make a profit you may have to pay **capital gains tax** (CGT). This is the tax you must pay when you make a profit on the sale of an asset.

Over to you

Can you name other assets on which you might be liable for capital gains tax?

The Stock Exchange and what it all means

The Stock Exchange is simply a market where shares are bought and sold. A company is said to have a Stock Exchange quotation when it has been given permission by the Stock Exchange to have its shares traded (bought and sold) on the exchange. A company can then sell its shares to the public and to financial institutions and in return acquire more funds (capital). A shareholder who buys shares and wishes to sell them later can sell their shares through the exchange.

Bulls, bears, and stags

These are people who speculate on the Stock Exchange in the hope of making money—like gambling. They hope to make a profit as a result of changes in the prices of shares.

A **bull** buys shares hoping they will rise in price, that is, buys at a low price, hoping to sell at a high price.

A **bear** sells shares at a high price in the hope of buying them back later at a lower price.

A **stag** buys newly issued shares, hoping they will rise in price.

Share prices rise and fall—why?

1 The size of the profits earned in the past and the profits expected to be earned in the future will affect share price.
2 Rumours about the company.
3 Plans for the company.
4 Changes in the rate of interest.

Can you think of any other factors that would affect share price?

Stock Exchange jargon

Take a look at the press cutting below: this is typical Stock Exchange information that you would find in the business section of a newspaper. It's not as difficult to understand as it may appear. Look at the translation that follows.

DUBLIN CLOSING PRICES							
TOP TEN COMPANIES 1	2		3	4	4	6	
Price	**% Change**		**Mkt**	**1998**	**1998**	**1998**	
(p)	**Wk**	**YTD**	**Cap(m)**	**Gr. Yld**	**P/E**	**High**	**Low**
AIB	980	-12.1	44.1	8412	2.4	16.0	1155	680
Bank of Ireland	1115	-9.3	3.0	5732	2.6	13.4	1590	1082
Elan Corp (Usc)	6475	-1.4	27.6	5120	0.0	33.4	7594	2775
CRH	770	-11.5	-6.3	2972	1.9	13.5	1125	770
Irish Life	555	-10.5	37.7	1737	2.9	15.0	716	400
Smurfit Group	135	-15.6	-31.8	1459	4.2	10.4	277	135
Kerry Group	800	-4.2	6.5	1360	0.7	17.7	1140	750
Ryanair	450	-9.1	35.1	753	0.0	20.4	615	330
Vindian Group Plc	551	-4.6	7.1	843	5.7	11.7	618	524
Independent	270	-16.9	-29.9	672	3.5	12.0	475	270
Top Ten companies	3079.0	-9.4	12.8	29062	2.1	15.9	3843.4	2729.9

Taken from *The Sunday Tribune*, Sunday 30 August 1998

1 Price

This is the price (in pence) for one share in the company at the end of the trading day.

2 % change

This is the percentage change in price per share

(a) over the past trading week (Wk) and

(b) over the trading year to date (YTD).

3 Mkt Cap (m)

This is *market capitalisation*, in millions—the market value of the company on the Stock Exchange. It can be worked out as follows:

Number of shares issued × Market price per share

4 Gr. Yld

This is the *gross dividend yield*—the annual dividend as a percentage of the share price. It can be used to compare the returns from different investments.

5 P/E

The *price/earnings ratio* indicates how many years it will take for the shareholder to earn back the money invested in it.

6 High

This is the highest price achieved by the share during 1998. 'Low' is the lowest price quoted for a share in the company so far in 1998.

Who is Dow Jones? When do they play FTSE on the Stock Exchange?

A **Stock Exchange index** gives a general indication of share price movements on the Stock Exchange. It is an average price of a sample of shares quoted on the exchange. If share prices in general are rising, then the index will be rising, and vice versa.

Dow Jones is not a person but the name given to the New York Stock Exchange index. Similarly, FTSE is not a game but the name given to the London Stock Exchange index.

Over to you

Can you name any other Stock Exchange indices?

Assignment

1 Can you remember the names of the main types of financial institutions? List them.

2 Project: Research the different investment options provided by each of the financial institutions. Prepare a summary report of your findings. Now you can make a more informed investment decision.

3 Star rating: Can you rate each of Aunt Aggie's suggested investment options for Mary Prendergast, using the following guide?

Excellent	★★★★★
Very good	★★★★
Good	★★★
Fair	★★
Poor	★

Complete the following table:

	Deposit account	Shares	Bonds	Property
Safety				
Access				
Return				

4 Neil Hanly wishes to buy a motorbike; it will cost him £250. He can save £5 a week in his piggy-bank.

(a) How long will it take him to save £250?

(b) Is a piggy-bank a good place for Neil to save his money? Why, or why not?

(c) Can you recommend an alternative?

5 What is the present rate of DIRT applied to most deposit accounts? Is it possible to pay a lower rate? How? Is there a catch?

6 Read the following newspaper item (which appeared on Saturday 30 January 1999), then answer the following questions:

(a) What is the name of the market where these prices arise?

(b) What is being priced?

(c) What was the price for Arnott's shares on Friday 29 January?

(d) Which of the shares has the highest price?

(e) Why do you think it is so?

Dublin Equities

High	Low	Capt. £m.	Company	Latest Price	Change onday	Change onWk.	Latest price£Rp	P/E Hist.	Div.Yld Gross%
1775	984	4,635.72	AIB	1700	−10	−25	1339	28.82	1.53
453	207	603.12	AWG	207	−3	−8	163	11.44	3.55
603	248	113.10	Abbey	292	+0	−8	230	6.79	4.89
1333	700	106.40	Adare Printing	700	−10	+0	551	7.60	2.32
272	170	690.41	Anglo Irish	258	−5	+3	203	17.52	2.66
273	140	57.97	Ardagh	170	+5	+10	134	7.39	4.68
838	648	127.04	Arnott	705	+0	−20	555	12.73	2.68
143	83	40.03	Athlone Extrusions	83	+0	−2	65.5	9.55	3.64
270	1	19.87	BCO Technologies plc	110.7	+0	+0	87	0.00	0.00
2100	1237	127.77	Bank of Ireland	1975	−30	−8	1555.5	21.88	1.66
127	70	130.36	Barlo Group	77	+0	+1	60.5	12.71	2.14
1573	940	5,558.40	CRH	1440	+29	+75	1134	22.57	1.20
1003	483	229.35	Clondalkin Group Unit	540	−10	−20	425	9.00	2.10
210	87	38.72	Crean (James)	88	−2	−5	69.5	3.50	13.14
902	432	688.37	DCC	790	+0	−5	622	17.39	1.73
311	220	21.79	Donegal Creameries	220	+0	+0	173	6.87	2.60
47	28	150.72	Dunloe Ewart	41	+0	−1	32.5	43.62	0.00
7294	2000	7,814.04	Elan Corporation	5888	+0	−122	4637	22.01	0.00
N/A	N/A	14.30	European Leisure	108	+0	+0	85	12.74	0.00
711	483	212.23	FBD	515	+0	+0	405.5	13.21	2.55
500	286	575.32	First Active	437	−3	−23	344	15.35	0.00
240	107	N/A	First Ireland	273	+0	+0	215	0.00	0.00
48	14	60.80	Fishers International	45	+0	+0	35.5	0.00	0.00
269	136	690.43	Fyffes	235	+0	+5	185	14.52	1.70
N/A	N/A	N/A	Galen Holdings	663	+8	+8	522	49.95	0.35
160	104	173.25	Golden Vale	110	+0	−2	87	10.78	3.05
2444	1346	256.32	Grafton Group	1600	+0	+50	1260	13.00	2.09
736	432	561.85	Green Property	503	−17	−34	396	31.52	1.46
579	267	650.76	Greencore	335	+0	−30	264	10.40	3.57
114	35	N/A	Hampden Homecare	60	+0	+0	47	7.60	69.50
336	175	88.12	Helton Holdings	190	−5	+5	150	9.34	3.68
1098	684	495.93	Hibernian	915	+5	−5	721	19.48	1.93
N/A	N/A	N/A	I.T.G. Group	590	+5	+25	465	68.63	0.00
425	210	409.96	IAWS	370	+0	−10	291.5	17.55	1.36
128	100	44.61	IFG Group	101.5	+0	+0	80	16.86	1.06
58	N/A	0.00	ILP Grp.	28.5	+0	+0	22.5	18.99	0.00
593	170	134.80	IWP Intl	170	−20	−40	134	5.18	5.49
597	273	834.15	Independent	340	+0	−10	268	12.93	3.12
1676	978	302.76	Irish Continental	1150	−25	−50	906	13.83	0.89
930	533	2,734.80	Irish Life	840	−35	−86	661.5	18.66	2.26
1490	889	1,351.48	Irish Permanent	1430	−15	−55	1126	26.97	1.57
279	165	13.88	Jones Group	267	+0	+0	210	18.68	0.00
851	552	288.60	Jurys Hotels	652	+2	+2	513.5	15.37	1.97
1448	927	1,978.58	Kerry Group	1150	+10	−45	906	22.99	0.54
444	218	412.90	Kingspan Group	250	+0	−15	197	13.87	0.62
N/A	N/A	N/A	Mackie	19(S)	+0	+0	15	0.76	56.95
508	2	81.90	Marlborough International	260	+0	+5	205	27.96	0.00
235	128	40.73	McInerney	162	+0	−1	127.5	12.63	0.78
N/A	N/A	N/A	Norwich Union	680	+25	+2	535.5	60.00	50.00
229	175	14.72	Norish	175	+0	+0	138	7.82	3.37
70	52	7.55	Oglesby and Butler	65	+0	+0	51.25	10.38	3.91
N/A	N/A	N/A	Powerscreen Intl	185	+1	+10	146	50.00	0.00
279	200	27.94	Qualceram plc	200	+0	−28	157.5	13.25	2.03
110	1	24.20	Rapid Technology Grp	110	+5	+10	87	16.64	2.39
220	130	139.10	Readymix	130	+0	+0	102.5	10.46	2.75
13	5	2.91	Reflex	7	+0	+0	5.5	2.23	0.00
127	75	63.08	Ryan Hotels	87	+0	−4	68.5	10.24	3.89
781	400	1,021.29	Ryanair	605	+21	+55	476.5	24.25	0.00
19	10	11.27	Seafield	17	+0	−2	13.5	18.89	0.00
65	36	34.89	Silvermines	38	+0	−3.5	30	8.44	4.79
352	110	1,577.99	Smurfit Group	145	−3	−13	114	13.21	4.58
132	89	7.19	Superule	118	+0	+0	90	16.64	2.39
381	160	32.67	Unidare	165	+5	−5	130	4.54	14.82
787	6	171.36	United Drug	680	+0	−10	535.5	18.46	2.31
157	67	541.98	Waterford Wedgwood	71	−3	−5	56	12.40	3.43

CHAPTER FIVE

Credit Where Credit Is Due

Financial management for the individual or business comes down to a balancing act: balancing income with expenditure. Planning or budgeting for the future helps to make sure your finances remain in balance. We all have needs and wants; but with limited funds we need to make careful decisions about how we spend our money.

Setting priorities

Household expenses can be divided into luxuries and necessities.

Over to you

Can you name *five luxuries* and *five necessities* a normal household might require each month?

From your list, can you identify items listed as necessities that people would have regarded as luxuries twenty-five years ago? Discuss.

Stretch your cash: wise buying

The task of balancing your income and expenditure can involve two approaches: increasing your income, or curtailing your spending. Options for increasing your income could include a part-time job, being paid for extra chores around the house, or turning a hobby or interest into a money-making enterprise.

Can you think of any other ways of boosting your regular income?

Also, by shopping around you can get better value for your hard-earned pounds. Remember, the less money you have, the more clever you have to be! Keep in mind the following steps to smart spending:

'At a great bargain, make a pause.'—
Anonymous

1 **Shop around.** Making the effort to compare prices can save you heaps.
2 **Look for 'Closing down' signs, bargain basements, or end-of-line sales.**
3 **Haggle.** It's worth a try! A loose button or a grubby mark may secure you a discount. Some shops even have a policy of matching any cheaper price you can find in another shop.

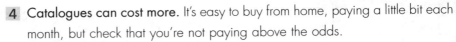

4 **Catalogues can cost more.** It's easy to buy from home, paying a little bit each month, but check that you're not paying above the odds.

5 **Be aware of the clever ways of making you spend more:**

- window posters screaming *'Sale,' 'Lowest prices ever,' 'Prices slashed'*
- shop assistants on commission: sales assistants sometimes earn more if they sell more. What are the implications of this?
- music, lighting, and surroundings—all geared to get you into that spending mode
- the positioning of stock: for example, freshly baked bread and cakes towards the front of the shop. Can you think of ways the aisle layout in a local supermarket might entice you to buy more?
- colour scheme: according to some people, different colours give out different messages. Yellow, for instance, signals cheapness; red, on the other hand, is said to trigger hunger pangs.

Yes, I'll take it ... How will I pay?

Go to Chapter 3

Most of the purchases you have made up to now have been paid for with cash. What other payment options are available to you? Can you think of an occasion when you had the use of a product or service without paying for it at that time?

Most people have bought on credit at some stage in their life—that is, bought now but paid later. You might not even have been aware of it. When was the last time you turned on a light, or the television or radio? ... Well, that was an occasion when you bought on credit!

Over to you

Get your hands on an ESB, gas or telephone bill.

- When did you use the electricity?
- When did you have to pay for it?
- How can you pay this bill?
- Did you get something free?—No, you did have to pay for it eventually, but not at the time of use.

'Accrued expenses'—unpaid bills—are a temporary source of finance and are a form of buying on credit.

Virtual money v. real money

Nowadays, 'plastic money' is taking over from cash as the most common method of payment, just as paper money took over from gold coins in the past. Some plastic money could even be described as 'virtual money', in that it has not yet been earned: it does not yet exist, but it can be spent.

Credit cards

With a credit card you are allowed to spend up to a certain amount; this is called your *credit limit*. Every month the credit card company will send you a bill for all the goods you bought using the card.

How is that credit limit decided? Does everyone get the same limit?

You must settle this debt within the credit period allowed, normally one month. If you don't clear the bill within this time, the credit card company will charge you interest on the money you owe. This is how the company makes a profit.

Is this the credit card company's only source of income?

Consumer tip

If you pay your credit card bill on time, the credit is free.

Charge cards

With charge cards—for example American Express and Diner's Club—you are given a credit limit; some even allow you almost unlimited spending, as with a 'gold card'.

An annual fee is charged to the customer for this card. You must pay the bill in full at the end of each month: the amount outstanding cannot be carried over to the next month.

Is everyone eligible for a gold card?

Store cards

These are issued by particular retailers—for example Clery's, Brown Thomas—to encourage customers to spend more in their shops. They can only be used in those particular shops.

The arrangements for payment vary among companies. Store cards may entitle you to discounts and to attendance at 'customer evenings' held in the shop.

Get thinking!

1. Why does a person take out a credit card or a charge card, when they know they must pay for the goods anyway?
2. What motivates a credit card company to give a complete stranger free credit?

Reasons for credit cards

From the customer's point of view, why get one?

- They allow you to buy more than your present funds allow.
- They are safer to carry around than cash.
- They are more convenient when you are buying expensive items and when booking over the phone.
- They allow for emergency purchases.
- They are sometimes requested as a form of security, for example when hiring a car or booking accommodation.
- They are international in use and trouble-free: most credit cards are accepted throughout the world, while the bills appear on your statement in your own currency.

From the provider's point of view, why provide a credit card?

- It encourages the customer to spend more.
- There is the opportunity to earn interest if the bill is not cleared by the end of the credit period.
- Income is earned by charging retailers for processing credit card transactions.
- An annual charge is earned on each credit card issued, regardless of the number of times it is used.

A sting in the tail ...

For the consumer, a credit card may encourage impulse buying, with consequent interest charges if the bill is not cleared on time. For the credit card provider there is a risk of bad debts: despite the careful vetting of a customer's creditworthiness, some credit card bills never get paid. Shopaholics beware!

Over to you

Can you think of any other drawback of credit cards?

Compile *five* golden rules that a customer should keep in mind before leaving home armed with a credit card.

A point to remember

'Plastic money' is a term sometimes used to describe **all** types of cards used to make payments for goods and services. As well as credit cards and charge cards, other common cards are ATM cards, cheque guarantee cards, and combined cards.

Over to you

Name the ATM cards provided by the various financial institutions. Can you name any other cards provided by financal institutions?

The methods of payment mentioned so far are suited to short-term, immediate needs. Long-term purchases—for example a house or a car—are better financed using long-term sources.

Borrowing

People borrow money because they lack the resources to buy expensive items, such as a house or a car. The type of finance you require depends on the goods you wish to buy and the life span of the item. For example, if you need to pay your annual car insurance but you have no money, where do you turn?

Because the insurance cover is for one year, in financial terms this is considered to be a short-term requirement. Would you use a fifteen-year loan to cover this expense? An unlikely option! Any expense that must be paid within a year should be financed by a short-term source. Suitable sources of short-term finance for a household are

- a bank overdraft
- a credit card.

Is there any other means of dealing with bills that arrive during the year? There is of course the system of 'accrued expenses', as mentioned earlier. How is this a source of short-term finance? Though we do not actually get money into our hand, by allowing bills or expenses to *accrue* or build up it frees our finances in the short term.

'Before you borrow money from a friend, decide which you need more.'—Anonymous

Over to you

We often encounter other expenses in life, such as buying a car or a house. Would it be wise or responsible to use a bank overdraft or a credit card to make these purchases? Justify your answer.

A good rule of thumb when borrowing

Match the financial need (short, medium or long-term) with the appropriate source of finance (short, medium or long-term).

Looking at medium-term finance

> Medium-term need (one to five years) ⇨ Medium-term source of finance

A car is usually bought with a medium-term source of finance (that is, one that must be paid back within one to five years). The main sources of medium-term finance for an individual are:

- personal loan
- hire-purchase
- leasing or renting instead of buying.

1 Personal loan (term loan)

The concept of a term loan is simple. The borrower is expected to work out the length of time for which they will require the loan; the lender and the borrower then tailor the loan to suit their requirements. The lender has some control over the money, as monthly repayments must be met. The borrower is forced to think through the project or idea to be financed before presenting it to a financial institution.

The time span of the loan is important: the longer you take to repay the loan, the more interest you have to pay.

Over to you

Tom can pay £122 a month over five years, or £157 a month over three years. Which repayment schedule would you recommend?

Where can I get a personal loan?

Personal loans are available from banks, building societies, and credit unions. Most financial institutions have developed extremely flexible loans that are adapted to suit the needs of the individual.

Can I be refused a personal loan?

Borrowing depends on many factors:

- the purpose of the loan
- the duration of the loan
- your annual income and occupation
- the size of the loan
- your security or collateral for the loan
- your ability to repay the loan
- details of other financial commitments.

If any of these don't measure up, you may be refused a loan.

Can you think of situations where a loan might be refused? Pick up a loan application form at a local bank and take note of the details they require.

Will the cost of the loan be the same in different institutions?

The rate of interest is the cost of the loan. The *annual percentage rate* (APR) is the effective rate of interest being charged on a loan, taking into account all the costs, including administrative costs. This is a standard measure of the cost of loans, hire-purchase deals, and other credit arrangements; it allows the borrower to compare the true cost of credit from different sources. All lending agencies are obliged by law to show the APR of their loans in their advertisements.

Under what law are companies obliged to give details of the APR?

Still confused?

If the APR means nothing to you, it is a good idea to ask the lender for the cost per month of each £1,000 borrowed. This figure can make more sense than a percentage interest rate like APR.

2 Hire-purchase

HP arrangements allow you to have immediate use of the goods, while paying for them in instalments over an agreed period. You have to pay a deposit at the beginning, and then a fixed amount in an agreed number of instalments. Only on payment of the last instalment do you legally become the owner of the goods.

Hire-purchase can work out more expensive than paying cash. Despite this, many households use the HP arrangement to buy household equipment and also cars. It is often used by people when they are unable to obtain any other form of loan.

Over to you

Make a list of possible purchases suited to a HP arrangement.

HP advertisements often appear in newspapers; collect three, and compare them.

3 Leasing or renting instead of buying

Leasing simply involves renting an asset; as a result, ownership never passes to the person leasing it. The leasing agreement also involves paying a deposit at first and then fixed repayments for the duration of the agreement. At the end of the period the goods are returned to the seller.

Leasing has considerable advantages: some arrangements include maintenance and repair of the goods, and the option of making a final payment to buy the goods at the end of the leasing period.

1 The cost of leasing can be considerably cheaper than HP. Can you think why this might be?

2 Advise Una Maloney on the best financial arrangement for the purchase of her new hi-fi system. Refer to Q.4 on page 43.

Looking at the long-term financial situation

Go to Chapter 6

Long-term needs (over five years) must of course be matched with a long-term source of finance. For the individual the biggest expense incurred during their lifetime is usually the purchase of a house. This is usually financed using a long-term source of finance (repayable over twenty years or more) called a *mortgage*.

Getting that loan

Problem page

Dear Aunt Aggie,

I have decided to build a conservatory at the back of my house. I've shopped around and received several estimates, the best of which is for £14,500. I'm writing to you to ask for your advice on how to finance this venture.

B. Clinton,

Ballybunnion.

Dear Mr Clinton,

1. Shop around! Think of financial institutions as financial supermarkets selling the product—money. It is important to get the best loan package—that is, the best interest rate, the best repayment schedule, and so on. This may involve making phone calls, writing letters, and visiting the bank.

2. Decide on the institution offering the best deal. Before going ahead with the loan, ask yourself the following questions:

   —Would it be wiser to save for the conservatory?

   —What is the real interest rate—the APR—to be charged on the loan?

   —What is the duration of the loan, compared with the expected life of the conservatory?

3. Complete the loan application form carefully.

4. In most cases it is necessary to visit the lender to talk personally to the lending official. Remember, the lender is trying to make sure that you are a safe bet for their money. From the point of view of the lender, there are three important issues here:

   - collateral—the security offered by the borrower for the loan: for example, the deeds of a house

   - capacity—the ability of the borrower to meet all the repayments

   - creditworthiness—the borrower's previous credit history; this will show how effectively loans were repaid in the past.

Remember, the burden is on you, the borrower, to prove you are a safe bet.

Aunt Aggie.

The 'three Cs'

Collateral

Capacity

Creditworthiness

> *Neither a borrower nor a lender be,*
> *For loan oft loses both itself and friend.*
>
> —Shakespeare

If you follow Aunt Aggie's words of wisdom, you should avoid losing 'itself and friend'.

Assignment

1. 'The wise borrower—there's no such thing: it's a contradiction in terms.' Discuss.

2. Identify occasions when careful borrowing is the right road to choose.

3 As well as basic foods, supermarkets stock unusual and luxury goods, which they hope you will see and buy. The layout of goods is therefore very important. Customers are made to pass by the non-essentials on their way to find what they came for.

(a) Draw a rough sketch of the floor plan of a local supermarket. What do you notice?

(b) Using the sample layout as a guide, decide on the best arrangement of the luxuries and the basics listed. What factors should you consider?

(c) The manager wishes to install three circular display stands around the supermarket to display the following items:

—cheap bumper-packs of beans

—luxury hand-made chocolates

—special Italian olive oil.

Add these to your plan, considering access for customers as well as the best place to position these items in relation to the other foods.

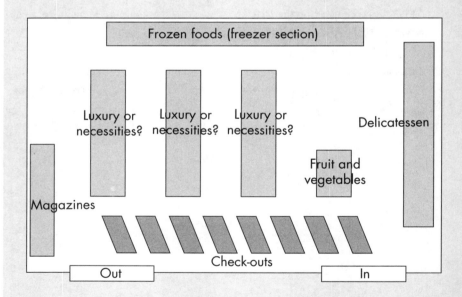

List of basics:	Fresh meat	List of luxuries:	Magazines
Bread	Frozen meat	Biscuits	Delicatessen
Milk	Fresh vegetables	Ready-made	Cut flowers
Tea and coffee	and fruit	meals	
Vegetables	Eggs	Wine and spirits	

4 Una Maloney has decided to buy a hi-fi system, which costs £345 in a local shop. She realises she has three options:

1. **renting:** £3.75 a week. As part of the arrangement, the seller will look after maintenance and repairs;

2. **hire-purchase:** there will be a deposit of £45 and instalments of £12 a month for four years. At the end of the four years the hi-fi can be purchased outright for a further payment of £20. Again as part of the arrangement the seller is responsible for the maintenance during the hire-purchase period;

3. **personal loan:** Una has saved £45 in the bank and has been told by the bank manager that she can borrow up to £300. She would have to pay £3.20 a month (which includes interest) for each £100 borrowed over a period of four years.

   (a) Which option is most cost-effective?

   (b) What other factors should Una consider before making her decision?

   (c) What other factors will the bank manager consider before sanctioning the loan?

   (d) The renting of an asset has another name. Can you think of it?

   (e) Once Una has bought the hi-fi system, what other costs might she incur?

5 Nessa is a university student and is going to America to work for the summer. When she approaches the student loan officer in the local bank for a loan of £1,000, she is refused. The loan officer explains that she could not possibly lend the money without some security (collateral). She suggests that a member of Nessa's family might act as guarantor.

(a) What is the purpose of having a guarantor?

(b) Can any member of her family act as guarantor? Perhaps her young brother Brendan could do the job.

(c) From the bank's point of view, is Nessa a good risk?

(d) Can you suggest other reasons why Nessa might be refused the loan? (Hint: the three Cs.)

CHAPTER SIX

Hey, Big Spender!

Don't be under any illusions! When you start earning, you may think you're in the money. Spending-sprees may be on the agenda, while the long-term effects of blowing your hard-earned money are ignored—a serious case of short-term gain (or pleasure) at long-term pain. Don't throw caution to the wind!

It's not necessary to take on the personality of Scrooge, but a little care is advisable. When you start earning money, the speed at which it leaves your pocket may take you by surprise. In this chapter we will look at the three main purchases in most people's lives:

—buying a car

—buying a house

—buying into a pension scheme.

Get motoring!

Edwina Jordan is getting on well in her new job in motor racing. However, she uses public transport to get to the race track and finds it frustrating. The main disadvantage is that the last bus on Friday is at eleven o'clock, and Edwina misses out on the social life her colleagues enjoy.

Over to you

Can you identify any other problems she might encounter using public transport?

She decides to buy a car. She is not sure whether to buy a new car or a second-hand car.

Over to you

What factors should Edwina keep in mind when making her decision?

Having considered her options, she decides to buy a second-hand car. Her cousins Rodney and Delboy give her the following advice:

● Is the mileage on the car legitimate? Some cars may have had the mileage gauge tampered with. Examine the wear and tear on the pedals: does it coincide with the mileage and the age of the car?

- How many previous owners were there? Many owners over a short period may suggest problems.
- Has the car been in an accident? Consider the amount and extent of damage. Colour can be a guide: is the colour of the car the same throughout?
- The interior of the car can give an indication of the way in which the car was kept.
- Consider the engine size; it could have cost implications in tax, insurance, and petrol consumption.

It's a good idea to get a reputable mechanic to check your potential purchase.

Over to you

Can you suggest where Edwina might find a second-hand car?

Where to look for the finance

Edwina has done her figures and needs to borrow £7,000 to buy the car. She has found the car most suited to her needs—and her limited resources. It is three years old, and she would like to repay the loan over a four-year period.

She has three options for financing the car. Can you name them? Which option would you recommend for Edwina, and why? Can you suggest where she will get the money?

It's not over yet!

Once the finance has been secured, there are other costs to be considered:

1 motor tax: this is a compulsory payment for the use of the road network;
2 motor insurance: it is compulsory to have third-party insurance;
3 running costs: the day-to-day costs of petrol, oil, anti-freeze and so on must be budgeted for. Other, less frequent costs include servicing of the car, new tyres, and so on.

Now you're motoring!

By securing the loan and meeting the repayments on time you are building up a rapport and a good credit record with the lender. This should lay the foundation for securing larger sums for possible future purchases—assuming you keep a clean slate with the bank that gives you the first loan, of course.

Home, sweet home ... Níl aon tinteán mar do thinteán féin

Marge and Homer are in love and have decided to settle down. They are not sure whether they should rent or buy a place they could call home.

Over to you
There are many pros and cons when buying or renting a house. Compare them.

Having looked at their options, Marge and Homer have decided to buy rather than rent. There is now another hurdle to overcome: the maze of options when deciding where to live:
—apartment or house;
—city life, suburban life, or rural life;
—new or second-hand;
—location: it's all about location, location, location.

Decisions, decisions, decisions
Homer is confused, and he consults the house-buyers' guide produced by Aunt Aggie's publishing company, where he finds the following tips.

1 Deciding on the property

Choosing the house of your dreams is a highly personal affair. You may opt for a three-bedroom semi-detached house in a housing estate, a bungalow in a rural retreat, a luxury apartment in a high-rise block, or a floating houseboat. The choice is yours; but there are certain things to keep in mind:
- Take a close look at the local amenities.
- Get a quantity surveyor to inspect the house and provide a structural report. This report should identify possible difficulties, such as structural damage to the property.
- A visit to the local planning office is advisable to see whether the property may be adversely affected by development proposals. Perhaps there are plans for road widening, which may lead to a compulsory purchase order (CPO) in the area.
- Talk to the neighbours and find out whether they have had any problems with the surroundings.

2 Agents

The purchase may require the services of an auctioneer or an estate agent. The role of an agent is to communicate between the buyer and the seller so as to agree the price of the property. The auctioneer is the agent of the vendor (seller), and their fee is paid by the seller. You can, of course, go it alone and sell your property without an estate agent, but remember that the agent can help take the pressure off by dealing with appointments to view the property and sorting out genuine bidders from the merely curious.

3 Conveyancing

The legal and administrative work involved in transferring the ownership of a property is known as *conveyancing*. The aim is to ensure that good title is acquired and that there are no restrictions on the use or enjoyment of the property. Buying and selling a property can be a very complicated procedure; solicitors are trained to carry out the transfer of ownership, and some banks are now providing this service.

Going to auction: Going, going ... gone!

The auction is a popular method of selling property when the property market is buoyant—though even then only properties in the higher price bracket are put up for sale under the auctioneer's hammer.

Generally speaking, you should only auction a property that is rather difficult to put a price on or that is likely to sell particularly well by reason of location or some other fact. For example, a house in Dalkey, County Dublin, was sold for over £6 million in 1998 but had a much lower guide price before the auction.

The principle of an auction is that two or more parties compete for the property, so one of them ends up paying a much higher price than might otherwise be obtained. It obviously achieved the desired effect with the house in Dalkey.

Over to you

Test your auctioneering skills

1. Read the property section of a newspaper over a number of weeks to get a feel for the present state of the property market.
2. Select a property that is going to auction, predict its sale price, and compare this prediction with the reality, i.e. the auction results.

The majority of home-buyers need to borrow most of the money they require. A *mortgage* is a loan taken out to buy a house or other property. It is usually the largest loan taken out by a person and is normally repaid over a period of twenty to twenty-five years. The property acts as security for the loan: the title deeds are given to the lender, so that if the borrower fails to repay the loan, the house can be sold by the lender to recoup the amount of the mortgage.

Financial institutions do not make a habit of reclaiming a house if repayments are not going according to plan. Why is this so?

The size of the mortgage will depend on the income and credit status of the borrower and also on the value of the property. Whatever type of home ownership you opt for, don't stretch beyond your means, or you may regret the move as you struggle to meet the repayments.

How much can I get?

The average mortgage is approximately two-and-a-half times the gross annual income of the principal earner. For a working couple, add on 50 to 100 per cent (depending on the financial institution) of the smaller salary. These are guidelines for calculating a mortgage: some institutions will give much more, depending on individual circumstances.

For example, here is a mortgage calculation for one working couple. The husband has a gross annual income of £30,000; the wife has a gross income of £35,000. What size of mortgage might this couple receive?

Two-and-a-half times £35,000:	87,500
Half of £30,000:	15,000
Total:	102,500

It would appear that this couple could get a mortgage of £102,500; but all is not as it seems! Based on their gross income, this couple could secure a mortgage of £102,500. They decide to buy a house for £80,00 and to use the 'spare' cash to splash out on a car, an exotic holiday, and a house-warming party.

Is it possible to organise your mortgage finance along these lines? Definitely not! The financial institution will only lend up to approximately 90 per cent of the value of the property being bought—regardless of the amount the borrower is technically eligible to receive.

In summary:

The size of the mortgage is dictated by the following guideline:

Annual gross income	*Value of property*
(2½ times principal earner	(Lenders will only lend up
+ ½ other earner)	to 90% of value of property)

Over to you

Why don't financial institutions give up to 100 per cent of the value of the property?

It's not over yet ...

Other costs that must be budgeted for when buying a house include:

- insurance—both property and contents insurance
- standing charges: electricity and gas bills, television licence, etc.

Go to Chapter 8

- maintenance—painting, repairs, etc.
- city life: if you are opting for an apartment, pay particular attention to the service fee payable by residents to maintain the building and grounds; the purchase of parking-space may also be necessary
- mortgage protection: it is advisable (and sometimes compulsory) to take out this type of life assurance policy, which on the death of the assured person will make funds available to clear the amount outstanding on the mortgage.

Go to Chapter 8

Preparing for your golden years: arranging a pension

Séamas Bond has worked for nearly ten years now and has paid pay-related social insurance (PRSI) during this time. The PRSI contributions are made to the state's funds and enable the state to provide a pension when he retires, and other benefits, which include the following:

- unemployment benefit
- maternity benefit
- widow's pension
- disability benefit.

(Obviously Séamas would not be entitled to all these benefits himself, but his wife might.)

The term *social welfare* is used to describe all types of benefits paid by the state.

The Pension Cake
Basic
↓
Deluxe
It all depends on the payments you make while working

Do I have to pay PRSI?

If you are employed, you must pay. When you reach the age of sixteen you will receive a PRSI identity card in the post, with your *Revenue and Social Insurance* (RSI) number on it. The Department of Social, Community and Family Affairs gives everyone a number, and this number will remain yours throughout your working life. This is so that a record can be kept of who has made their PRSI contributions, and exactly how much.

PRSI entitles you to a basic pension, called a contributory state pension. If you have not worked, you are still entitled to a pension—called a non-contributory pension.

A case in point

Séamas Bond is concerned that his life will change dramatically once he retires and that his state pension won't adequately allow him to participate in all the activities he normally enjoys. His personal assistant, Maura Moneypenny, has advised him that unless he gets his financial act together he will suffer a huge drop in income when he retires. She gives him the following advice:

When planning your financial future, you have three choices:

1 invest your money;
2 take out a life assurance policy;
3 arrange a pension plan.

Pension planning—the sooner the better

The longer you delay starting your pension arrangement, the more it will cost you to provide a reasonable pension. The younger you are when you start your pension payments, the more years you will have (until you reach sixty-five) to spread out your contributions. This will, of course, lower the contributions you will have to pay.

The moral is 'Don't delay!' Indeed, if you leave it too long the cost may become prohibitive, and the only option will be to settle for an inadequate pension.

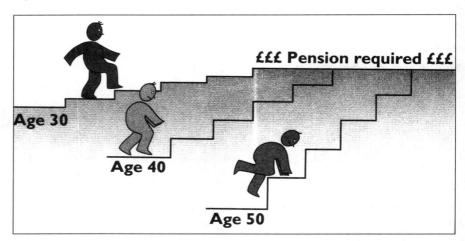

CHAPTER SEVEN

Let the Buyer Beware

The butcher, the baker, the candlestick-maker, film stars, rock singers, models, football-players, and you—all have something in common: you are all consumers.

Over to you

Can you identify goods and services that each of these people consume?

Though we all consume goods and services regularly, we are not always sure what to do when things go wrong.

Problem page

Dear Aunt Aggie,

Can you help me? Yesterday was my birthday and I bought a pair of 'Tiger' runners. I wore them all day, and I noticed last night that the sole of one of the shoes had started to fall off. I need your advice.

Teresa,

Tullamore.

PS: It was my father's fault: he wouldn't let me buy my favourite brand.

Dear Aunt Aggie,

Last week I bought a coat in a local department store. There was a sign on the stand saying '100% pure new wool.' When I came home I noticed that the label read '60% pure new wool, 40% acrylic.' I was very disappointed, as I had paid a lot of money. What should I do?

Mossie,

Mullingar.

Dear Aunt Aggie,

It was my mother's birthday last week, and I bought her a bright-blue skirt. Unfortunately my mother doesn't like bright blue, so I decided to return it to the shop. They refused to exchange the skirt or give me a refund. Can you give me some advice, please?

Carmel,

Castleknock.

Over to you

Assume you are Aunt Aggie. What advice would you give to these dissatisfied customers?

Unsure? Well, take a look at the following laws.

Consumer legislation

Laws (also called *acts* or *statutes*) are passed by the Dáil for many different reasons. The following laws have been introduced to give protection to citizens when they act as consumers:

The Consumer Information Act (1978)—what it means to you

- It prohibits false or misleading statements regarding
  —the description of goods;
  —the description of services;
  —the indication of prices;
  —advertisements;
  —claims made through pictures, catalogues, or oral statements.
- Any information about the product, given directly or indirectly, is considered a description. It may be given by means of a picture on a package, or an oral statement by a salesperson.
- Goods in a sale must have been on offer at the pre-sale price for twenty-eight consecutive days in the previous three months.
- The act established the Office of the Director of Consumer Affairs, which has to pursue sellers who break this law.

Take note

The Consumer Information Act does not give any rights to customers but tries to protect them by imposing certain duties on the retailer.

Examples of false description would include

- a shop with the sign 'Open 24 hours' that closes at 2 a.m.
- a holiday brochure that states 'Beach five-minute walk,' but it takes thirty minutes to get there
- a builder advertises 'No job too small,' but when asked to build a dog kennel he refuses, saying, 'It isn't worth my while.'

Over to you

Have you come across any other examples of false descriptions?

The Sale of Goods and Supply of Services Act (1980)

1 Goods must be of 'merchantable quality'.

2 If the buyer relies on the seller's skill and judgment, the goods must be reasonably fit for the purposes intended.

3 Goods bought by description must correspond to that description.

4 Goods bought by sample must correspond to that sample.

5 The supplier of a service must have the necessary skill to provide that service. Materials used must be sound and of merchantable quality.

6 If a substantial fault is discovered soon after the goods have been bought, the customer may be entitled to reject the goods and claim a full refund, if they act promptly.

This act and you

1 'Merchantable quality' means good quality relative to the price paid.

2 You buy a computer printer, having relied on the expert advice of the sales assistant. You attempt to print your end-of-term project, only to find that the printer is not compatible with your computer.

3 You buy a pair of shoes that are described as waterproof, yet when it rains your feet get wet.

4 Your mother buys ten rolls of wallpaper based on a sample seen in the shop. The sample has orange flowers on a white background. When she brings the wallpaper home she finds to her dismay that the wallpaper has the orange flowers but on a black background.

5 Driving your newly serviced car home, you notice that the car is pulling to the left, and the brakes don't work very well.

Over to you

Now empowered with this information, can you advise the troubled consumers?

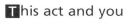

What to do when things go wrong

1 Return to the shop where you bought the item—ASAP!

2 Complain to the right person, that is, someone who can remedy the situation.

3 Pick the right moment: it could greatly improve your chances of success.

4 Be polite: don't lose your temper.

5 Explain your problem and suggest possible remedies. (Be reasonable and realistic.)

6 Keep in mind the responsibility of the seller to you.

7 A letter of complaint may be necessary.

8 Keep a copy of all documents—receipts, correspondence, etc.

Stating your case

Sometimes a letter of complaint is the most effective approach. When you are writing letters of complaint it is necessary to be brief and clear. Aunt Aggie suggests the following letter for Teresa regarding her runners:

Teresa's address

> 13 River Street
> Tullamore
> Co. Offaly

14 July 1999

The right person —

Where Teresa bought the runners

The Manager
Sportsco
Main Street
Tullamore
Co. Offaly

Dear Sir/Madam,

What was bought, and proof of purchase

State the problem

On 12 July I bought a pair of 'Tiger' runners for £56.95 in your shop (copy of receipt attached). After wearing them for one day, I noticed that the sole of one of the shoes is coming apart.

Why doesn't Teresa send the original receipt?

State the desired remedy

Under the Sale of Goods and Supply of Services Act (1980), these shoes are not of merchantable quality, and I would be obliged if you would let me have a full refund of the price.

Yours sincerely,
Teresa Talbot

Redress: you know the problem—what's the solution?

Under the Sale of Goods and Supply of Services Act (1980) you may be entitled to one of three things:

The three Rs

—a refund;

—a replacement;

—a repair.

Caveat emptor—Let the buyer beware!

If the goods have been used, or if you delay in complaining, you may be entitled only to a part-refund or to a repair. You have no rights—

- if you change your mind
- if you abuse the goods
- if faults were pointed out by the seller or should have been discovered by you on examining the goods before purchase.

Don't be fobbed off!

It is the seller who is responsible for putting things right. Signs that imply that you have no rights—e.g. 'No refunds,' 'Credit notes only will be given'—are *illegal*.

A guarantee is an *extra* benefit and does not affect your rights under the law.

Don't give up!

If you're still unsuccessful having followed the guidelines above, and you feel you have a genuine cause for complaint, help is at hand.

1 Trade associations

Some retailers are members of organisations that represent their trade, such as the Irish Travel Agents' Association and the Society of the Irish Motor Industry. These organisations may give you a hearing and be of assistance.

2 The Consumers' Association of Ireland

The Consumers' Association provides the 'Consumer Personal Service', which, for a fixed payment,

—examines the problem and advises on the best course of action;

—undertakes liaison with the supplier;

—if it is appropriate, takes legal action.

3 Office of the Director of Consumer Affairs

This is a state agency whose role is to provide information to the public about consumer protection and also to inform traders of good practice. There are offices in Dublin and Cork, and others will open shortly in Limerick, Athlone, and Sligo.

4 The Small Claims Court

Established in 1991 at various centres around the country, this service at present costs the consumer only £6, but claims are limited to a maximum of £600. By paying a small fee and completing an application form, the aggrieved consumer is provided by this court with a speedy resolution without the usual legal delays. Each court has a *small claims registrar*, whose job it is to help consumers with the paperwork involved in making a claim.

5 The last resort: taking legal action

Remember that taking this route will cost the consumer time, money and energy and should be avoided where possible.

Remember

Though the laws are there to protect you and give you rights, you have a responsibility to protect yourself by being a careful customer. Let the buyer beware!

Assignment

1 In each of the following cases,

(a) state whether in your opinion the customer has cause for complaint;

(b) if yes, state which law has been broken;

(c) say whether you think the customer is entitled to redress;

(d) if yes, state which type and why;

(e) say what you think they should do.

1. Clíona buys a hairdryer. She plugs it in, and it doesn't work.

2. Aisling buys a pair of jeans. The label reads 'hard-wearing'. On the first day she wears them, they rip at the knee

3. Emer buys a carton of her favourite yoghurt in a local shop. At home she notices that the expiry date has lapsed by a fortnight.

4. Donagh buys three yards of fabric in a sale. It was marked 'shop-soiled'. On arriving home he finds that half the fabric is faded.

5. Ann buys a pair of red shorts for her holiday. When she brings them home she doesn't like the colour.

2 Liam Brown went on a school tour recently and visited his favourite team's sports ground. While there, he bought a jacket and paid £85 for it. However, when he put it on he discovered that the zip wouldn't work. He decided to write to the manager of the shop. He wants his money back but is not sure whether he should send the receipt.

(a) Has he a right to complain? Why, or why not?

(b) Has any law been broken?

(c) If yes, which aspect of the law in particular has been broken?

(d) Do you think he is entitled to a full cash refund? Why?

(e) Should he accept a credit note?

(f) Should he include the original receipt in his letter?

(g) Assume that you are Liam Brown, Ballybofey, County Donegal. Write a letter of complaint to the Manager of ABU Sports Shop, Carlow Street, Dublin.

3 Sometimes retailers give refunds and replacements though there is nothing wrong with the goods—for example when the customer has a change of mind. Why do they do this if they don't have to?

4 Why are sellers more likely to want to give credit notes than refunds?

5 Many of the larger retailers have 'customer service desks' in their shops. In your opinion, why have they started this practice?

6 Some companies have drawn up 'customer charters'.

(a) Identify a company that has a customer charter.

(b) Investigate what it contains.

(c) Do you think it is in the interest of customers?

(d) Can you suggest any improvements to it?

CHAPTER EIGHT

Safeguarding Your Crown Jewels

Insurance is simply a way of reducing the risks that are part and parcel of everyday life. In the seventeenth century, many firms went out of business when their premises burned to the ground. An accidental fire caused by a candle or a spark would ruin the business and would put many people out of work.

Gradually it began to occur to people that they could share the loss caused by the risk of fire if they each paid in a certain amount every week or month, and this money was used to help the few people who actually experienced a fire. This is called 'pooling the risk'.

Ship-owners in the seventeenth century developed the insurance concept. The owners met in Edward Lloyd's coffee-house in London and insured their ships and cargoes before voyages. Those whose ships were lost received compensation from the pool of money contributed by all the owners.

Insurance today

Insurance now covers many items and events, such as houses and horses, storms and ships, accidents and works of art, defective products, holidays and hotels, even actors' faces and footballers' legs. Bewley's of Grafton Street have insured their specially commissioned windows for over £1,000,000.

The insurers use *actuaries*, who work out the probability of any event happening and then use these figures to set the *premiums*—the amount paid to get insurance cover.

Example

An actuary might establish that for every thousand households there is likely to be one major fire, causing approximately £100,000 of damage, each year. If a thousand householders want insurance cover for fire, then the company will charge them about £150 a year. These premiums will bring in £150,000 in a single year.

How insurance works

Premiums	→	Insurance	→	£100,000 will cover risk of a claim
£150 p.a.	→	pool:		
per household	→	£150,000	→	£50,000 for the insurance company

Over to you

1. What do you think the insurance company will do with the £50,000 safety net?
2. What happens if more than one household makes a claim for compensation this year? What is the best and the worst outcome from the point of view of the insurance company?

Insurance and assurance

Many different types of insurance are available today, but there is an important distinction between the two major types, *insurance* and *assurance*.

Insurance is a scheme that covers you for something that may or may not happen. You pay premiums that are not refundable, so that you are insured if the event you fear happens, for example a burglary or a car crash.

Assurance is a scheme that covers you for something that definitely will happen, usually your death or your reaching a certain age, whichever comes first. The policy's 'lump sum' will be paid out in each case.

Risks all around me ... so what do I insure?

A general rule is that you should insure anything that might cause you financial hardship if it were lost or damaged. In fact insurance companies insist that you have an *insurable interest*, that is, a financial relationship with the object or person being insured, and that you would suffer financially by its loss. Most households insure their assets and insure themselves against personal risk.

Insuring your assets

House insurance covers both the building and the contents in the event of damage caused by fire, water, accident, or burglary. *Mortgage protection insurance* is another type of house insurance that is necessary nowadays.

Insuring your health and safety

People spend huge sums of money insuring themselves against risks that may or may not happen. A wide range of insurance packages is available.

Take note

Insurable interest —a principle of insurance

Personal accident insurance provides compensation if you have a serious accident. It is often taken out by holiday-makers before travelling abroad.

Health insurance provides protection against the costs involved in medical treatment.

Over to you

Can you name the providers of health insurance?

PRSI

This is the state pension scheme, whereby employees contribute a proportion of their pay (hence the name *pay-related social insurance*) and as a result are entitled to a wide range of benefits: unemployment benefit, health benefit, and so on. It is compulsory for employees to contribute to PRSI; the contribution is usually deducted by the employer on behalf of the state from the employee's wages.

PRSI is a statutory deduction from your pay packet. Can you name another?

Critical illness cover

Critical illness cover provides protection against the loss of income suffered as a result of a serious illness. Benefits paid out under these policies do not necessarily have to be used to pay hospital bills.

Life assurance policies

Life assurance policies are taken out for two main reasons:

Go to Chapter 4

- to provide protection for the next of kin in the event of the assured person's death
- as a means of saving.

There are three main types of life assurance policy.

- *Whole-life policies* pay out only when the person dies.
- *Term policies* pay out if the person dies within a specific period.
- *Endowment policies* pay out when the person reaches a certain age, say sixty-five, or dies before the age of sixty-five, whichever comes first. It is therefore a combination of life cover and investment policy for a given number of years.

Over to you

1 Find out the types of policies taken out in your household. For what reasons were they taken out?

2 'Insurance frauds are at the root of some of our most notorious cases,' says Detective-Sergeant O'Carroll. What does she mean?

Motor insurance

There are three types of motor insurance.

1 Third-party insurance

When a person with third-party insurance is at fault in an accident, the insurance company will pay compensation to those injured—the 'third party' (the first and second parties are the insurance company and the person who took out the policy). Third-party insurance is the most basic form of car insurance, and is compulsory in Ireland .

Over to you

Why do you think it is compulsory?

2 Third-party, fire and theft insurance

Third-party, fire and theft insurance compensates the third party and also compensates the insured person for loss arising from the theft of the car or for damage resulting from fire.

3 Comprehensive insurance

Comprehensive insurance covers all people and cars involved in an accident and any incidental damage to the insured person's car. Even if the insured driver is at fault, their insurance company will pay compensation to all injured parties, including the policy-holder.

1 Which policy offers the best cover?
2 Which do you think would work out to be the cheapest?

The insurance family photo

The *insurance agent* works for one insurance company and tries to sell insurance on their behalf.

The *actuary* calculates the premium to charge the insured person, based on statistics and the probability of that risk occurring.

The *assessor* is sent out by the insurance company to assess the damage and decide how much money the company will agree to pay out as compensation.

The *broker* listens to what the customer requires by way of insurance cover, then uses their expertise and experience to find the best deal to cover that risk. The broker shops around and is paid commission by the insurance company that gets the contract.

The *insured* is the person covered by the insurance policy.

The *insurer* or *underwriter* is the company willing to provide cover on specific risks. It 'underwrites' the value of the item to be insured.

Arranging that insurance: the step-by-step guide

1 **Find the best quote.** Insurance companies sell the same basic product—insurance cover—and compete vigorously to obtain new customers. By shopping around you can secure the best deal: the best premium, extras, etc. Some insurance companies have a company policy of matching competitors' quotes.

2 **Apply for insurance.** To obtain insurance cover, it is necessary to complete an application form, known in the insurance world as a '**proposal form**'.

3 **Agree the premium.** The premium—the price charged by the insurance company to cover you against the stated risk—depends on

The premium can change each year if the level of risk has changed.

- the value of the item to be insured
- the age of the item or person to be insured
- the number of people seeking insurance for a similar risk; the greater the number of people paying in to a particular fund or 'risk pool', the lower the premium each must pay
- the number of claims by that person or for that risk
- the location of the item to be insured: for example, motor insurance is more expensive in Dublin than in other areas
- a good record: insurance companies reward people who do not make claims by offering a discount on their premium—this is called a '**no-claims bonus**'.

   In summary, the higher the risk to the insurance company, the more expensive the insurance cover will be for you.

4 **Sign the contract.** Details of the agreement between the insurer and the insured are contained in a document called the *insurance policy*. A renewal notice is sent out to remind the customer when the next premium is due. *Days of grace* are sometimes allowed—extra days of cover allowed by the insurer, which gives the tardy customer time to renew their policy. Motor insurance policies are not allowed any **days of grace**.

Disaster strikes—what to do

Contact the insurance company to obtain a *claim form*. Fill it in completely, honestly, and accurately. An assessor will come to inspect the damage, and shortly thereafter you should receive compensation.

Problem page

Dear Aunt Aggie,

I bought a set of golf clubs in June 1999 for £800. They are my pride and joy, and I insured them at that value. I had only had them for eighteen months when they were stolen from the house. I followed the normal procedure when making a claim and found to my dismay that the insurance company will only give me £650 as compensation. I have tried to explain that my clubs cost me £800 and were insured for £800 and that I expected to get the full £800 as compensation. According to the insurance company, I would be making a profit if they were to give me £800. They mentioned something about indemnity, which I don't really understand, and I think they are trying to pull the wool over my eyes.

Paul Harrington
Portmarnock,
Co. Dublin.

Aunt Aggie replies:

Hard luck, Paul! Your situation illustrates a very important principle of insurance: *indemnity*. This simply means that you cannot make a profit from insurance. Though your clubs did cost you £800, their resale value eighteen months later would *not* be £800. The insurance company has assessed the value of your clubs as £650. In effect, they are saying to you that you should be able to buy eighteen-month-old clubs for £650. If they were to give you £800 you would in fact be making a profit. The aim of insurance is to put you back in the position you were in before your goods were lost or damaged, not to enable you to make a profit from the mishap.

A general point to note when renewing insurance policies: make sure you place a realistic value on the item insured, because there is nothing to be gained from over-insuring your assets.

Take note

***Indemnity*—a principle of insurance**

Problem page

Dear Aunt Aggie,
Following a car accident, in which my car was completely written off, I received £4,000 compensation. I intended to sell the written-off car, but my insurance company stopped me in my tracks. They told me that they were now the owners of the car. Is this true?

Deirdre Hill
Mondello Road,
Dublin.

Aunt Aggie replies:

As you have received full and adequate compensation for the loss suffered, you should now find yourself in the financial position you were in before the accident. If you were to hold on to the wreck and sell it later, you would be further gaining, or profiting, from your insurance policy. Having paid out the compensation, the insurance company becomes the legal owners of the wreck. This is known as subrogation—another principle of insurance.

Problem page

Dear Aunt Aggie,

I've insured my car for £8,000 with two insurance companies and paid a premium of £500 to each. I was involved in an accident where £3,000 of damage was done to my car. I claimed for £3,000 from each company. However, the insurance companies delayed compensating me, as I mentioned while making the claim that I had a second insurance policy on my car. At the end of the day they accepted that I had done this in innocence and offered to pay me £1,500 each. Have I been short-changed?

Bríd Mackey
Cavan.

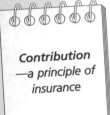
Aunt Aggie replies:

This is an interesting case. Had each insurance company given you £3,000, you would have ended up with £6,000 compensation for £3,000 damage, thereby making a profit of £3,000. This represents a breach of the indemnity principle. To prevent this happening on a large scale, the principle of contribution was introduced by the insurance industry whereby the insurance companies only pay compensation that restores you to your original position.

The wise consumer's guide to insurance

1 Read the policy

It may seem obvious, but many people each year are disappointed—and a lot poorer—because they did not read the details of the policy. For example, some household contents policies do not have specific cover when you take, say, a portable radio or personal stereo out of the house. Such **all-risks insurance (ARI)** usually requires a specific arrangement, and an additional premium to be paid.

2 When you have carefully read the policy, file it safely.

3 Take out adequate cover

If you under-insure assets, you will lose out if they are destroyed.

The Murphy family own a computer worth £1,000. However, it has only been insured for £500—half its value—because this would work out cheaper in premiums. In the event of a burglary they will receive only £500 compensation. In the insurance industry this is known as the '*average clause*': that is, compensation is paid in proportion to the insurance cover: half insured, half compensated; one-third insured, one-third compensated, and so on.

4 Complete honesty

The customer who fails to mention when filling in a motor insurance proposal form that he is a part-time rally driver will risk losing his right to compensation if he writes off his car while racing at the weekend. This is known as the principle of *utmost good faith* in insurance.

In summary, there are five basic principles to be kept in mind when taking out insurance:

1. insurable interest
2. utmost good faith
3. indemnity
4. subrogation
5. contribution.

Take note

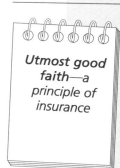

Utmost good faith—a principle of insurance

Business insurance

Large compensation claims and unexpected disasters could lead to the end of a business and the loss of many jobs—unless the business has taken out insurance cover to protect against these risks. As well as insuring against damage or loss to company property (like the household), there are other policies that are particularly important for a business.

1 **Public liability insurance** covers a business against claims by members of the public because of the activities of the business or accidents on its premises.

Over to you
Can you think of any company that has been sued because of the ill-effects of its business activities?

2 **Product liability insurance** provides cover against claims for harm or loss suffered through the use of the firm's products. In recent times, cigarette companies are in the news because of claims made by the public.

What is the nature of these claims?

3 **Employers' liability insurance** provides protection for employers against claims made by employees as the result of accidents, injuries or illness suffered at work. Members of the army have made successful claims against their employer—the state—for damage to their hearing while in military service.

Can you think of any other cases where the employer was sued by an employee as a result of injury caused at work?

4 **Consequential loss policies** cover a business against loss of profit as a result of a temporary closure caused by, for example, a fire.
5 **Fidelity guarantee insurance** provides cover against dishonesty or fraud. For example, it would protect a business against the loss of trade secrets when an employee goes to a competitor.
6 **Key person insurance** protects against the loss of valuable employees who may be regarded as the 'key' to the success of the business.

Employers must also pay compulsory pay-related social insurance (PRSI) for each employee in their employment. The employee, as you know, also makes a compulsory contribution.

Assignment

1 Jack and Vera Doyle have recently bought their first house, by means of a mortgage from a building society. They paid £85,000 for the house, and they have spent £15,000 on furnishing it. They are now wondering about insurance, and ask for your advice.
(a) Are they required by law to insure the house?
(b) Having shopped around, they have obtained the following quotes:
  (i) Sure Bet Insurance Company: 20p for each £100 of building insured; 90p for each £100 of contents insured.

(ii) All-Star Insurance Company: £2.50 for each £1,000 of building insured; £7.50 for each £1,000 of contents insured.

(iii) Trouble-Free Insurance Ltd: 30p for each £100 of building insured; £6.50 for each £1,000 of contents insured.

Which is the cheapest quote?

(c) Is the cheapest quote always the best option?

(d) Some insurance companies offer a discount if the person seeking insurance takes steps to reduce the risk. Suggest steps that Jack and Vera might take.

(e) Help Jack and Vera complete the proposal form on the following page, having selected the cheapest option.

(f) Name the principles of insurance that Jack and Vera should keep in mind when completing the proposal form.

(g) Jack and Vera think the premium is very expensive, especially for the contents. They are now thinking of insuring the contents for £12,000: they don't see the point of insuring them for their full value. Advise them on the implications of this decision.

(h) Show what compensation they would receive if they insure the contents for £12,000 and if, as a result of an electric heater accidentally left on all night, £2,000 worth of furniture was destroyed.

(i) Suggest other policies that Jack and Vera should consider.

2 Distinguish between

(a) insured and insurer;

(b) actuary and assessor;

(c) broker and agent;

(d) policy and proposal form;

(e) premium and compensation;

(f) whole-life and endowment assurance.

Spot the difference

3 Look at this drawing, then answer the following questions.

(a) Was car A or car B responsible for the accident?

(b) Who has to pay for the repairs to the cars if both drivers have only third-party, fire and theft policies?

(c) Who pays for the repair of a car with third-party insurance if it hits a wall?

AIB Insurance Services
Ashford House
Tara Street
Dublin 2
Customer Services Helpline 1850 27 26 25

Your Proposal for
AIB Home Insurance

AIB Home Insurance has been specially negotiated for AIB Bank customers and provides high quality cover. It is underwritten by Guardian PMPA Insurance Limited and full details of the cover are contained in the policy, a copy of which is available on request.

Important Note: You must give full and true answers to all questions. If you do not do so, your insurance cover may not protect you in the event of a claim. If you are in any doubt whether certain facts are material, please telephone our Customer Services Helpline on 1850 27 26 25. You should keep copies of all correspondence in connection with this Proposal.

FOR BANK USE ONLY (Please complete in BLOCK CAPITALS)

AIB Branch _____ N.S.C. | 9 | 3 | | | | | Sales ID | | | | | Staff Name _____
Policy No. _____ Sector Code | | | | | Lead ID | | | | | Staff No. | | | | | |

Please complete in BLOCK CAPITALS

Section 1: Personal Details

Surname

First name(s)

Title *(Mr, Ms, Mrs, Miss)*

Date of Birth

Postal address

Address to be insured *(if different)*

Contact telephone number 9am-5pm

Occupation – First Applicant

Home telephone number

Occupation – Second Applicant

Section 2: Description of Property

Is this property a Private Residence ☐   Investment Property ☐   Holiday Home ☐   B&B/Guest House ☐

• If **Private Residence**, is it used for business or professional purposes other than clerical business use?   Yes ☐   No ☐

   If **YES** please give details

• If **Investment Property**, state number of tenants *(Max. 10)* ☐ • If **Holiday Home**, do you rent it out?   Yes ☐   No ☐

• If **B&B/Guest House**, state the number of guests you can accommodate *(Max. 10)* ☐

Section 3: Cover Date

When is the insurance cover to begin? **Buildings**   Date _____   **Contents**   Date _____

Section 4: Buildings *(Minimum Sum Insured £40,000)*

Is cover required?   Yes ☐   No ☐   If **YES** state **Sum Insured** £ _____

Is there any other financial interest in the building *(eg Bank, Building Society)*   Yes ☐   No ☐

If **YES** give name and address _____

Section 5: Contents *(If Buildings cover is chosen, your contents will be covered for an unlimited amount provided your Buildings Sum Insured does not exceed £300,000. However, this does not apply to Investment properties).*

State value of your Contents if over £50,000 as there will be security requirements £ _____

• If Buildings cover is **not chosen** or if this proposal is for an Investment Property please state the Contents sum insured   **Sum Insured** £ _____

• **Specified Valuables** – please specify any valuables worth more than £2,000 per item *(Note - Valuables are jewellery, watches, gold or silver items, furs, cameras (which includes camcorders), binoculars, paintings, collections of stamps, coins, medals)*

Description	Sum Insured £	Description	Sum Insured £

• **Accidental Damage to your Contents** *(additional premium will apply)*

   Is cover required?   Yes ☐   No ☐

CHAPTER NINE

The National Purse-Strings

A budget

A budget is a financial plan. It is a plan of what you expect to earn, and how you plan to spend the money. What is the aim of a budget? Why should people budget?

The **national budget** is the financial plan for the country—but there is a difference: you know how much you will earn, and then you decide how you will spend your earnings. However, the Government decides how much it wants to spend, and then decides where to get the money.

Over to you

How does the Government earn money? What does it spend it on?

The work of the Government is divided out among its members, called **ministers**. Each minister is responsible for one **department**.

The department, along with the minister, has to decide how much money it will require for the year—this is called an **estimate**. These estimates are sent to the Department of Finance, where they are discussed; and when they are completed the **book of estimates** is published.

Over to you

Complete this table naming the various Government departments, and name the minister responsible for each department.

Department	Minister
Department of Finance	
Department of Education and Science	
Department of	
Department of	
Department of	
Department of	
Department of	
Department of	
Department of	
Department of	
Department of	
Department of	
Department of	
Department of	
Department of	

In your opinion, does each department receive the amount of money it requests? Why, or why not?

The book of estimates forms the basis of the budget, which is introduced by the Minister for Finance. In addition to the various Government departments making demands, the Minister for Finance is also lobbied by **interest groups.** These include the Irish Business and Employers' Confederation (IBEC), the Irish Farmers' Association (IFA), the Small Firms Association (SFA), the Institute of Taxation, etc.

The Irish National Organisation for the Unemployed lobbied for an increase in tax-free allowances before the 1998 budget.

Over to you

What issues might these interest groups put forward to the minister? Can you think of other interest groups that lobby the Government, and what they might be looking for?

In the period immediately before the next budget, scan the newspapers to find out who wants what, and why.

The two Cs

The national budget is divided into two parts:

● the current budget
● the capital budget.

current   **>**   current
income   expenditure

The current budget

This is the part of the national budget that we are most familiar with. It is concerned with income earned on a day-to-day basis and money spent on day-to-day

£100m   £80m   expenses.

If current income equals current expenditure, the current budget is said to be *balanced.* If current income is greater than current expenditure, there is a *budget surplus.* If current income is less than current expenditure, there is a *budget deficit.*

current   **<**   current
income   expenditure

Over to you

1 Give examples of how the Government might earn its current income.

2 Give examples of current expenditure the Government might have.

£100m   £120m

3 If you were the Minister for Finance, what would you do with a current budget surplus?

4 As Minister for Finance, how would you handle a current budget deficit?

The capital budget

This is the other part of the national budget. *Capital expenditure* means spending on items that will last a long time, for example sewerage systems, hospitals, schools, or roads. The *capital income* used to finance this type of expenditure is usually obtained through borrowing; it is from this borrowing that the *national debt* arises.

Over to you

1 Can you give any other examples of capital expenditure?

2 Can you suggest how these items might be financed? (Hint: selling the crown jewels of the country.)

The national debt

The national debt is the amount of money owed by the Government for present and past borrowings. At present it stands at over £30,000 million. *Servicing* the national debt—that is, paying the interest—is a burden in itself, which is exacerbated by the fact that the Government still borrows more money every year.

Over to you

1 If you were the Minister for Finance, what would you do to reduce the national debt?

2 How does the national debt affect the ordinary taxpayer?

Assignment

1 (a) When you are planning your personal finances for a year, what are

  (i)   your main sources of income and

  (ii) your main items of expenditure?

  (b) Can you classify your items of expenditure as

  (i)   current expenditure and

  (ii) capital expenditure?

2 Here are the Government's main sources of current income:

- customs duties
- excise duties
- income tax
- corporation tax
- value-added tax (VAT)
- car tax.

Which is the greatest source of income? Rank the others in order of size.

Go to Chapter 10

3 Here are the principal areas in which public money is spent:

(a) health

(b) education

(c) social welfare

(d) Defence Forces and Garda Síochána

(e) interest on the national debt.

Starting with the largest, rank them in order.

4 For each of the following Government departments, can you

(a) name three items of current expenditure?

(b) name three items of capital expenditure?

—Department of Health and Children

—Department of Education and Science

—Department of Enterprise, Trade, and Employment

—Department of Justice, Equality, and Law Reform

—Department of Social, Community and Family Affairs.

5 To raise extra finance, the Government usually increases the price of petrol, alcoholic drinks, and cigarettes. Find out how these items have been affected in the most recent budget.

6 Why do you think the Government is inclined to increase the price of the items mentioned above? These items are described as 'price-inelastic' products. Can you think why?

CHAPTER TEN

It's a Taxing Life

Mention the subject of tax to most people and you'll be guaranteed a reaction. It would be an exceptional person who hands over a chunk of their pay packet and hasn't got strong feelings on the matter. Down through history, the taxing of incomes has often been viewed as unfair, and tax collectors were not held in high esteem. On the other hand, people expect the state to provide a range of services. Health, education and social welfare are nowadays considered basic state services. What about hospitals, street lighting, the Gardaí and the dozens of other services essential to modern living?

Who will foot the bill? The taxpayers, who are the main source of funds the Government uses to finance these services.

Over to you

Can you identify other services provided by the state? Make a list of the main types of tax levied at the present time. Can you identify other sources of finance available to the Government?

In a modern state, the Government also uses tax as a means of altering the distribution of income. The state helps those who need help at the present time.

The rules of the game

Every effort has been made to make the tax system as fair as possible. The system is founded on the principles put forward by the economist Adam Smith in his book *The Wealth of Nations* in 1776, which are still widely accepted today. He proposed four basic principles:

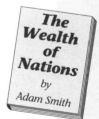

The
Wealth
of
Nations
by
Adam Smith

1 **equity**: equality of sacrifice, that is, each taxpayer should pay tax in proportion to their ability to pay;

2 **certainty**: the taxpayer should know how much tax they have to pay;

3 **convenience**: tax should be collected from taxpayers at a convenient time; the PAYE system allows tax to be collected in the most convenient way for the taxpayer;

4 **economy**: the costs of assessing and collecting tax should be reasonably small compared with the amount of revenue the tax brings in.

In addition to these principles, modern economists would add the following:

- People should be taxed so as to achieve a proper distribution of incomes.
- The tax system should not act as a disincentive to work or to discourage investment.

Over to you

1 Do you think it is easy for governments to operate a tax system that incorporates all the principles of taxation mentioned above?

2 Do you think the present tax system conforms to Adam Smith's principles of taxation?

3 'The more wealth you have, the more tax you should pay.' Discuss.

The tax maze

The following are the main types of tax levied on individuals and households at the present time:

- pay-as-you-earn (PAYE) income tax
- value-added tax (VAT)
- deposit interest retention tax (DIRT)
- motor tax
- local authority taxes or service charges
- excise duties.

Over to you

1 From the list above, can you name the biggest source of income for the Government?

2 Can you name any other taxes?

3 Do we have to pay taxes?

Tax in Ireland can be classified into three basic categories:

- tax on income
- tax on expenditure
- tax on capital.

A closer look ...

1 Income tax: the PAYE system

Income tax was introduced to Ireland in 1853. Throughout the nineteenth century, income tax was used mainly to finance wars, and the rate of tax was low. By the late nineteen-twenties, for every £1 of income earned, 15p was contributed as income tax. As the needs of the state grew, so did the rate of income tax levied on its citizens.

In 1960 an important change in the application of income tax took place, when *pay-as-you-earn* (PAYE) tax was introduced for most workers. This system allows for the deduction of income tax at the source, that is, from the pay packet received by the worker. The rates of tax are decided each year by the Government in the national budget.

Note: The tax year begins on 6 April and ends on 5 April the following year.

A map of the income tax maze

Denis Trump has done very well while on transition year work experience and has been offered a summer job.

'Make sure you get your tax situation in order' were the last words his employer said before Denis returned to school. 'If you have your tax-free allowance sorted out before you start working in June, you'll avoid paying emergency tax.'

Though Denis was a business studies whiz in Junior Cert, he is a bit confused about his tax situation. 'Emergency tax' sounds serious, and Denis wants to be organised before starting his first job. He comes to the conclusion that it can't be all that difficult, since other workers caught in the 'tax net' have come to grips with the system.

Before Denis consulted his sister Aoife, a tax expert, he made a list of some questions he needed answers for.

1 What are tax-free allowances?

Your tax-free allowance, as the name suggests, is that part of your income that is not taxed. The amount depends on your personal circumstances. It is made up of various allowances and *reliefs*, such as married person's personal allowance, mortgage relief, etc.

Believe it or not, the tax office is aware of your existence, even though you may never have been in contact with them. Around the time of your sixteenth birthday you will receive a card in the post—not a birthday card, but a type of tax birthday card. It will have your Revenue and social insurance (RSI) number printed on it, and this will act as your tax identity number for all future dealings with the Revenue Commissioners.

My tax questions
1. What are tax-free allowances?
2. How do I get them?
3. How will my employer know?
4. Emergency tax
5. Do students pay tax?

Don't worry if your RSI number is late arriving: the tax office can sometimes run behind when posting new cards. But if you need your RSI number in a hurry or before you turn sixteen, you can always phone the tax office, and they will have a record of the number.

Go to Assignment 1 page 79

2 What must I do to get my tax-free allowance?

When you start work for the first time, complete form 12A and send it to the local tax office. The details provided by you on this form will be used by the tax office to calculate the tax-free allowance you are entitled to receive, and the rate of tax that will apply.

A few weeks later you will receive a *certificate of tax-free allowances*. This will set out in detail your allowances and the tax rate that applies to you. Your RSI number will also be given.

3 How will my employer know the correct rate of tax to deduct from my pay packet?

The Revenue Commissioners will send the appropriate details to your employer, so that you are taxed only on your taxable income.

4 Emergency tax—it sounds painful. What is it, and how do I avoid it?

If the tax office has no information about your circumstances, the correct tax allowances cannot be decided. If you don't get around to sending in form 12A before you start your first job, you will have no tax-free allowance and the tax office will charge you, for the time being, more tax than you would normally pay.

In summary:

No planning, no form 12A filled in, and therefore no certificate of tax-free allowances received: neither the tax office nor your employer knows your correct tax status … Emergency tax for you!

So, just because I'm a little disorganised I'll lose out by having to pay more tax?

Well, yes, but only for a short while.

Emergency tax will be refunded; but there could be a delay, during which time you are out of pocket.

5 I'm told students pay no tax. Could this be true?

Yes and no! A student (or any other person, for that matter), having entered the tax system and having had tax deducted during their summer job, faces a possible windfall: a tax refund when the summer job has ended.

Anyone who works for only three months of the year is unlikely to have used up their complete tax-free allowance by the end of their summer job. In effect, they haven't earned more than their tax-free allowance and therefore don't fall into the tax net. So money deducted during the summer months is now refunded to them. It's worth your while investigating this, as it could mean big money!

Calculating your tax liability

Assuming you are now settled in your new job, the next question is: How is income tax calculated?

Denis has started in his summer job, and all was going well until he received his first pay packet. He was told that his weekly gross earnings would be £120, and, though well aware that some tax would be deducted, he was surprised by the amount he actually got to take home. He asked Aoife to go through his pay slip with him.

Percentage of taxable income / Percentage of gross pay

Name	Pay			Tax-free allowance	PAYE	PRSI dues	Union	VHI deductions	Total pay	Net
	Basic	OT	Gross							
D. Trump	120.00	—	120.00	62.00	15.08	6.60	1.00	—	22.68	97.32

To help Denis understand his pay slip, Aoife did the following calculations. Can you follow them?

1

Gross pay	120.00
less tax-free allowance	62.00
Taxable income	58.00

2

Tax rate: 26%

Tax rate × taxable income = tax paid:

26% of £58 = £15.08

3

PRSI = $5\frac{1}{2}$% of gross pay

= £6.60

4

In summary:

Gross pay		120.00
less deductions:		
PAYE	15.08	
PRSI	6.60	21.68
Net pay		98.32

Paper, paper everywhere ...

Some other tax forms you might come across include:

P60

At the end of the tax year (5 April), the employer gives form P60 to each employee. It shows the amount of pay and the total income tax and PRSI deducted from it for the tax year.

P21

You can request form P21—an *income balancing statement*. This will compare the tax paid with the amount that should have been paid. This statement could bring to light an overpayment of tax, in which case a refund will be made to you by the tax office. But be warned! This statement could also draw attention to an underpayment of tax on your part.

P45

If you leave your job you will receive a *cessation certificate* or form P45. This gives details of your gross income earned up to now, tax deducted, and other deductions. Form P45 can be used when claiming social welfare benefits or reclaiming tax; if you start in a new job it is handed to the new employer so that they know the rate at which they should deduct tax from you.

2 VAT—a tax on expenditure

For most purchases, either of goods or services, a proportion of what you pay goes to the state. This is called *value-added tax* (VAT). Unlike PAYE, this tax can be avoided, by not buying highly taxed goods: the more luxurious the item, the higher the rate. Some goods and services are exempt from VAT: these include certain food and drink (such as milk and bread), some books, and medicine.

There are at present two rates of VAT that a householder will encounter:

- $12\frac{1}{2}\%$ certain fuels (coal and gas), newspapers, etc.
- 21% (standard rate)—all goods and services that are not included in the other categories.

VAT is collected by the retailer on behalf of the Government and is sent to the Revenue Commissioners every two months.

Once we have decided to buy the item, we have no choice but to pay the VAT: it's included in the price.

3 Capital taxes

There are essentially two capital taxes that might affect an individual:

1 **Capital gains tax (CGT):** this is a tax on any profit from selling an asset, such as property or shares. However, there are exceptions, including gains made from selling a house if it is the family home.

2 **Capital acquisitions tax (CAT):** this is a tax paid on gifts or inheritances of substantial value. The relationship between the giver and the receiver will affect the amount of tax levied.

Go to Chapter 4

Assignments

1 Imagine you are starting your first job.
  (a) Complete form 12A to obtain your certificate of tax-free allowances. Refer to pages 80 and 81.
  (b) Some information may be required to complete the form. Where might you obtain it?

2 Brian Boylan, a computer operator, worked 48 hours last week. His basic pay (gross) is £140 for a 38-hour week; overtime is paid at £6 an hour. His tax-free allowance is £65 a week. His income tax rate is 26 per cent; PRSI is $5\frac{1}{2}$ per cent. Other deductions include union dues of £2.45 and VHI of £5.
  (a) Calculate his net pay (using the old tax allowance system).
  (b) Now design a pay slip for Brian. Make it as clear and easy to understand as possible.

FORM 12A

IF YOU ARE COMMENCING EMPLOYMENT IN THIS COUNTRY FOR THE **FIRST TIME,** USE THIS FORM TO :

Register for Social Insurance Purposes
and
Apply for a Certificate of Tax-Free Allowances

PERSONAL DETAILS

☐ Mr.   ☐ Mrs.   ☐ Miss.   ☐ Ms.   Please tick (✓) appropriate box

Surname   N1 . . . . First Name(s) N2 . . . .

Address   N5 . . . .
. . . .

If you already hold an RSI Number enter it here   ☐☐☐☐☐☐☐☐
[**Note:** all persons aged 16 years or over
have been given an RSI Number by The Department of Social Welfare].

If you do **NOT** hold or know your RSI Number, please give the following details:

Your Nationality . . . . Date of Birth . . . .
Your Pre-marriage name (if different from above) . . . .
Mother's Pre-marriage Name . . . .

Marital Situation - Are you ?   Single   Married   Widowed   Married and living apart

Please tick (✓) appropriate box   ☐ K1   ☐ K2   ☐ K3   ☐ K1/K2

If you are married, please give the following information in relation to your spouse:
Pre-marriage Name(if different from above) . . . .
First Name(s) . . . . Date of Marriage . . . .

If you are widowed, please state date you became a widow(er) . . . .

SOCIAL INSURANCE REGISTRATION

Social Welfare Pension, Benefit or Allowance. If you receive any of these, please state:

Type of Payment . . . . Amount per week £ . . . .

Date Present Employment Commenced . . . . Your Occupation. . . . .
Name & Address of Employer . . . .
. . . .
Employer's PAYE Registered Number . . . . Unit No . . . .
Social Insurance Class applicable to your employment . . . .
(ask your Employer, if necessary)
Employer's Trade/Profession . . . .

Are you related to your Employer by marriage or otherwise?   ☐ Yes   ☐ No   Please tick (✓)
If you are related, please state the relationship . . . .

If you were insured in any other EC country or in the Isle of Man, please state:

Country in which you were employed . . . . Insurance/Registration No. . . . .
Date of taking up/resuming residence in this country . . . .

REMEMBER TO COMPLETE THE REVERSE SIDE

APPLICATION FOR FIRST CERTIFICATE OF TAX-FREE ALLOWANCES

Please give the following information: Tick (✓) the appropriate box

                             per week ☐

The amount of your Pay £ . . . .   per fortnight ☐

                             per month ☐

[Note: in addition to wages/salary, Pay includes the value of all benefits (whether paid in kind or in cash) received by you from your employer - e.g. company car, living accommodation, luncheon vouchers, incentives, personal expenses paid by employer (e.g.VHI or other insurance premiums paid by employer) etc.]

Other Income   Description . . . . Amount £ . . . .

(e.g.Dividends, Interest, ... Amount £ . . . .

Rents, Trade, Farming,etc.) . . . . Amount £ . . . .

If married, give details of your spouse's income:

From Employment (if any) £ . . . .

From Other Source(s)   £ . . . .   Give details . . . .

You will be given the appropriate Personal Allowance, PAYE Allowance and PRSI Allowance, where due.

Mortgage Interest Relief -If you have a mortgage, state: amount of mortgage £ . . . .

                                when taken out . . . .

                           current rate of interest . . . .

Medical Insurance Relief - State amount of your yearly premium, if any £ . . . .

Other Allowance Relief (if you consider you are entitled to any other allowance / relief, give details)

. . . .

. . . .

[Information Leaflet IT 1 (available from any tax office) lists the main allowances and reliefs available]

PLEASE NOTE

There are heavy penalties for giving false information or for claiming allowances/reliefs that are not due.

DECLARATION

I declare that all of the information given by me on this form is correct to the best of my knowledge and belief.

Signature . . . . Date . . . .

Telephone No. . . . .

Please complete and return this form to me as soon as possible.

When returning this form, use any envelope and write **FREEPOST** over this address.

➡

OFFICE HOURS
Monday to Friday
9.30 - 12.45
2.00 - 4.00

3 Mary Regan, an engineer, worked a basic 38-hour week. She is paid £4.40 an hour, with overtime at time and a half. Last week she worked 47 hours. Her tax-free allowance is £70 a week. She pays PAYE at 26 per cent, and PRSI at 5½ per cent. Her other weekly deductions are: union subscription, £4; VHI, £6; and pension contribution, £10. Make out Mary's pay slip.

4 Neil Hanly, an office manager, works a basic 38-hour week, with overtime paid at £9 an hour. His last week's partially completed pay slip is shown below. Read the pay slip, then answer the questions that follow.

Name	Pay			Tax-free allowance	PAYE	PRSI dues	Union	VHI deductions	Total pay	Net
	Basic	OT	Gross							
N. Hanly	200.00	45.00		95.00			6.00	14.00		

(a) What was his gross pay for the week?

(b) How many hours' overtime did he work?

(c) How much of his pay was taxed?

(d) Calculate his PAYE contribution at the rate of 26 per cent.

(e) Calculate his PRSI contribution at the rate of 5½ per cent.

(f) What were (i) his total deductions and (ii) his net pay?

Budget 1999

—A radical change to the tax system

*The 1999 budget has been hailed as the most radical for years, because of the decision of the Minister for Finance, Charlie McCreevy, to move into **tax credits** and away from the old system of allowances.*

Question: What exactly are tax credits?

Answer: The best way of explaining tax credits is by reference to the old system of allowances. Take John, a single man with no mortgage earning £15,000 a year. Assuming a personal tax-free allowance of £3,950, this means that £11,050 of his income was subject to tax. Of that £11,050, the majority was subject to tax at 24 per cent and a small amount subject to 46 per cent tax.

However, under the tax credits system, John is taxed on the full £15,000—again the majority subject to tax at 24 per cent and the rest at 46 per cent. At this point John's 'credits' against that liability kick in. Allowances that he is due are multiplied by the basic rate of 24 per cent, and this credit is set against the tax liability.

Question: So why were the budget's tax measures regarded as radical?

Answer: A cynic might suggest it is because the notion of tax credits is not widely understood. In reality, what is radical is the scrapping of the old system of allowing allowances and reliefs at the top rate of tax. It is this, together with the increases in tax-free allowances and tax bands, that is having an impact on the bottom line of your pay packet. Introducing the system of tax credits as it exists now merely involves a change in the way your tax liability is calculated.

Question: What is the practical impact of the budget measure?

Answer: Take the old system, and, for the sake of simplicity, assume there were two tax rates, of 25 per cent and 50 per cent, according to Tony Walsh of Matheson Ormsby Prentice. If the minister had £300 million to spend on reducing the tax burden through increasing tax allowances, those paying at the top rate of tax would receive £200 million of the benefits, and those paying at the standard rate would get the remaining £100 million. Under the new system, everyone would get a tax credit at the 25 per cent rate; therefore the tax benefit of £300 million would be equally divided between the standard-rate and top-rate taxpayers.

The person on low wages gets the same benefit from allowances plus VHI and mortgage reliefs as a high-earner. To put it another way, every £1,000 of an allowance is worth £240 (based on the present standard rate of 24 per cent) to each taxpayer.

Question: If the old system of allowing reliefs and allowances at a higher rate (46 per cent) has been scrapped, did the top-rate taxpayers not lose money in the budget?

Answer: It is true that reliefs and allowances are now only allowable at the standard rate of 24 per cent, instead of 46 per cent, for high-earners. If this had happened in isolation, higher-earners would have seen a huge increase in their tax liability.

But to compensate for this, the minister sharply raised the level of allowances and significantly widened the tax bands. Personal allowances have been increased by £1,050 (double this for married couples) and the lower tax band increased by £4,000 to £14,000 (again, double this for married couples).

While this protected high-earners and ensured that they will make some gains from the budget, it also ensured that the largest tax-cutting budget in the history of the country was mainly focused on the lower-paid.

Question: Is the new system more equitable?

Answer: Yes. Because the reliefs are only allowable at the standard rate, everyone gets the same monetary benefit from their allowances and reliefs. However, there is an opposite viewpoint. Not only do higher-earners pay more tax in real terms, because their salaries are higher, but at least part of their salaries is taxed at the higher level. If they have to pay tax at the 46 per cent rate, is it not fair that they should also receive reliefs at the top rate?

Potential problems would also arise later if the Government needed to increase tax rates. In such an event the higher-earners would be massively hit.

A Government could, of course, opt to reduce tax-free allowances; but would it then be accused of equally hitting the rich and the less well off?

Question: Will there be further changes in the move towards a tax credit system?

Answer: The minister has already said that there are some small measures to be addressed in next year's budget to complete the change-over, for example the introduction of tax credits for certain groups that have constitutional as well as legal implications.

There is concern that a future budget may seek to reduce relief for pension contributions to the standard rate, which would mean that pensions would cost a lot more to finance.

A full implementation of a system of tax credits would involve the introduction of a basic allowance payable to every citizen. Whether or not future Governments will be willing to embrace such a radical step remains to be seen.

Compiled by Shane Coleman, *Sunday Tribune*, 6 December 1998.

A closer look at some pay packets under the tax credits system

Lisa, a single woman earning £20,000 and living in rented accommodation. Take-home pay increases by £30.08 per month.

	Old Tax System		New Tax Credit System	
	1998/99		**1999/2000**	
	Income		Income	
Salary	**20,000.00**		**20,000.00**	
Less personal allowances and reliefs:				
Personal allowance	3,150.00			nil
PAYE allowance	800.00	3,950.00		nil
Taxable income		16,050.00		20,000.00
Tax at 24%	2,400.00		3,360.00	
Tax at 46%	2,783.00		2,760.00	
		5,183.00		6,120.00
Less credits:				
Personal allowance			4,200.00 at 24%	−1,008.00
PAYE allowance			1,000.00 at 24%	−240.00
Rent relief		120.00		−120.00
Net income tax payable		5,063.00		4,752.00
Add PRSI and levies:				
PRSI	666.00		666.00	
Levies at 2¼%/2%	450.00		400.00	
Total PRSI and levies		1,116.00		1,066.00
Total income tax, PRSI, and levies		**6,179.00**		**5,818.00**
Net annual income		**13,821.00**		**14,182.00**
Net monthly income		**1,151.75**		**1,181.83**

Richard and Niamh, two young professionals, have an increase in their net income of £56.50 per month. They are claiming full mortgage interest relief.

		Old Tax System		New Tax Credit System	
	1998/99	**1999/2000**			
		Income		Income	
Salary		**50,000.00**		**50,000.00**	
Less personal allowances and reliefs:					
Personal allowance	6,300.00			nil	
PAYE allowance	1,600.00			nil	
		−7,900.00		nil	
		42,100.00		50,000.00	
Tax at 24%	4,800.00		6,720.00		
Tax at 46%	10,166.00		10,120.00		
		14,966.00		16,840.00	
Less credits:					
Mortgage interest credit		1,200.00	1,200.00		
Personal		nil	2,016.00		
PAYE		nil	480.00	−3,696.00	
Net income tax payable		13,766.00		13,144.00	
Add PRSI and levies:					
PRSI	1,710.00		1,782.00		
Levies at 2¼%/2%	1,125.00		1,000.00		
Total PRSI and levies		2,835.00		2,782.00	
Total income tax, PRSI, and levies		**16,601.00**		**15,926.00**	
Net annual income		**33,399.00**		**34,074.00**	
Net monthly income		**2,783.00**		**2,839.50**	

Compiled by Ann Williams, manager of KPMG Personal Financial Services.

You in Business

CHAPTER ELEVEN

Entrepreneurs—
Born or Bred?

A bank official becomes a leading player in the world of formula 1 racing. An RTE cameraman achieves success in the creative field of hand-made pottery. From a humble corner shop a leading light in the grocery trade emerges. The list continues …

Each of these people is now running a highly successful business.

Over to you

Can you identify the success stories mentioned above?

What is the common factor?

There are many motivations for starting up in business:

- the pursuit of an interest or development of a hobby
- the desire to be one's own boss
- the desire to become rich
- necessity—if a person finds it difficult to get a job or is made redundant.

These are some of the motivations for setting up in business; but successful entrepreneurs have certain qualities or characteristics:

- drive and energy
- a strong belief in themselves and in their idea
- vision
- determination
- a passion to be a success and for their business to succeed.

When all is said and done, there is no standard formula. Drive, passion and a will to survive make up some of the essential ingredients in the recipe for success. So it could be you!

If there is one thing that identifies a potential entrepreneur it is the attitude summed up by George Bernard Shaw when he said, 'You see things and say, "Why?" but I dream things that never were and say, "Why not?"'

You don't have to own and run your own business to be enterprising. There are many people who have no desire to go the whole hog and to set up in business but are quite enterprising in their present work. They prefer the role of managing a business in an enterprising and exciting way, rather than setting up and running their own. 'Intrapreneurship'—being enterprising within an existing business—is recognised and rewarded by many organisations. The ESB is an established supporter of intrapreneurship and has rewarded its employees' bright ideas. Another well-known product—'Post-It' notes—originated in an employee's idea in a large American company. Can you name the company?

Remember, there is a role for everyone, and a business might not survive if there were too many entrepreneurs and not enough managers and workers.

Please remove the rose-tinted glasses!

Don't be under any illusions: being your own boss is hard work. At the end of the day, when everyone else goes home, the business is your 'baby' and may be the cause of many sleepless nights. It also involves taking risks—in money, energy, time, and possibly career commitment.

If at first you don't succeed, dust yourself off and try again. As in all things, there is a learning curve involved; there is as much to learn from failure as from success. The number of failures under your belt need not be viewed as a negative thing: it can even be viewed as a valuable learning experience.

Get the connection

Before you embark on your mini-enterprise, ask yourself: have you got what it takes? Remember, at the end of the day:

'The only place where success comes before work is in a dictionary.'

CHAPTER TWELVE

The Idea

Identifying the right product or service at the outset will help in the success of your business; and it is not as difficult to find as it may appear.

Over to you

Look around you. Look at yourself!

What are your hobbies? What are your skills? Is there a business opportunity waiting for you in your own area?

Helping with the search: the alternatives

1 **Buying an existing business.** A word of caution: don't take on a business that involves a high degree of expertise. By the time you become skilled in the job, the business opportunity may have passed you by.

2 **Management buy-out.** This is when a group of employees buy the business they have been working in from the owners. It is usually done as a last resort to keep the business going. When Tesco decided to enter the retail grocery market in Ireland, the route they took was to buy an existing chain, Quinnsworth. However, they were not interested in taking over the sports and leisure division; and, rather than see the business close, the management undertook a management buy-out.

3 **Inheriting a business.**

4 **The tried and tested route: becoming a franchise-holder.** This means setting up a business using an already successful formula: a recognised name, an established image and reputation—like the Body Shop, McDonald's, Supermacs, Bewley's. Becoming a franchise-holder enables you to tap into existing goodwill.

5 **Import substitution.** This means making a product in Ireland that is at present being imported: it could be described as 'piggybacking' on an existing idea.

6 **Filling a gap.** Many successful businesses arise from filling a gap in the market, though the product or service may or may not be a new idea.

Go to Chapter 21

A fresh start

Can you identify a gap in the student market in your school?

7 **Opportunity knocks.** Change provides potential entrepreneurs with lots of opportunity: changes in the age profile of the population, life-style, and other demographic issues. What products or services have emerged as a result of these changes?

8 **Staying ahead of the posse!** Trying to identify future trends may bring to light possible business opportunities.

9 **Inventing a completely new product or service.** Q4U is a fresh approach to resolving an age-old inconvenience. This new Dublin firm will 'queue for you' for a small fee when you wish to renew your passport or your motor tax, when you need something urgently but you're too busy to queue.

Over to you
Can a new product be copied?

How can you protect your new business idea?

1 Patent
A patent prevents others from copying your product. To register your patent (and ultimately protect your earnings) you must pay a fee, which will protect your business from copy-cats. An annual fee must be paid to retain your patent.

2 Trademark
This is a recognised mark, in words or pictures, that distinguishes your product or service from others. As with a patent, you must register your trademark and pay an annual fee to retain it.

Over to you
Think of products or companies that are easily recognised by their trademark.

3 Copyright
This provides protection for creative work—paintings, writing, films, or music. No formal registration is required, but the onus of proving ownership lies with the creator of the work in the event of a dispute.

It's all in the name
Securing a good product or service is important, but equally important is choosing an apt business name. This name may help to sell your product, as it will have an impact on the minds of your potential customers and conjure up certain images for them. Some business names have become so well known that we tend to call all

similar products by the business name of their first manufacturer: for example, Hoover is the name of one company, but many people use that name to describe all vacuum-cleaners.

Over to you

Can you think of any others?

The road to success

The road to success can be mapped out in the *business plan*. Research suggests that more than 70 per cent of business failures are caused by a lack of planning. If the essential stages of the business are planned, it will be easier to implement them.

The business plan will include sections on

- background to the business
- the management team
- market research
- marketing
- finance for the business
- projected sales, expenses, and profit.

Go to

mini-enterprise business plan, page 92

Sample business plans are available from regional enterprise boards, providers of finance to business, and other organisations. Most businesses must prepare a business plan to accompany their loan application when seeking finance. Planning your business should be a continuous process, not just something you do at the start-up stage.

Get the connection!

1 Product or service—where do we start?

- Talk to family and friends for suggested ideas.
- Browse through newspapers and magazines.
- Surf the net.
- Hobbies or skills might kick-start your imagination.

Doing some of this kind of research will make it easier to come up with ideas. Follow up this research with a 'brainstorming' session. Consider all suggestions; the craziest ideas might trigger sound and profitable businesses. Lightning might strike!

Metalwork products

Christmas decorations

Babysitting service

Salad dressings

Producing a play

Woodwork products

School stationery

Hand-made chocolates

Tuck shop

Before you finally decide, do a reality check.

- Can we make it?
- Have we the necessary resources and skills?
- If we haven't, can we get them?
- Is the product or service seasonal: will it leave us high and dry at certain times of the year?
- Can we be competitive?
- Are we in danger of infringing a copyright, patent, or trademark?
  Even if you've considered all these aspects, the most crucial question is:
- Can we sell it?

'The glory went to the man who invented electricity, but it was the man who invented the electricity **meter** *who made the money.'—Anonymous*

2 Choosing a name

Now that you've a brilliant idea, you need a catchy name. It could be the key to your success.

A mini-enterprise that produced salad dressings was called 'Dressed for Dinner'. Another example is the group of enterprising pupils who sold personalised cloths (and hooks) to hang by the blackboard—not to clean the board but to keep hands dust-free. The name? 'Chalk Busters'.

Over to you

Use a brainstorming session to come up with an appropriate name for your business.

A business name can be used on printed letter-headings and business cards and for advertising. Business cards are a useful and cheap way of advertising. You can leave them with your customers as reminders. A trade mark or a logo might also be useful, as it gives instant recognition to your business.

Having chosen a business name and perhaps a logo, design the layout of your business card.

3 Your business plan

In your mini-enterprise a business plan is also useful, and may take the following form. Some of the following chapters will help you to complete your business plan.

Our business

This section introduces the business and includes the following information:

Names of the pupils involved

Their role in the business

The business name

The product or service—a description

Information about those consulted in the preparation of the plan

Market research

Proof of demand for the product

Who are your potential customers?

Who are your competitors?

Can you identify your *unique selling-point* (USP)?

Production

Production target

Number of production hours available

Details of requirements for the product: raw materials, equipment, facilities, skills, etc.

Quality control

Description of the production process

Marketing

Selling price of the product or service

Where will you sell your product or service?

How will you promote your business?

How much do you intend or need to sell?

Finance

How much is required to get the business operating?

Where will you get the money?

Keep an eye on the cash: prepare a cash flow forecast.

Over to you

Complete the 'Our business' part of your business plan. Remember, the business plan speaks for you and your business when you're not around.

CHAPTER THIRTEEN

Knowing Your Market

I keep six honest serving-men
(They taught me all I knew);
Their names are What and Why and When
And How and Where and Who.

—Kipling

The business may have chosen what it believes to be a brilliant idea; but before embarking on the project they need to examine a few issues.

- Is our proposed product or service **what** the customer wants?
- **Who** will buy the product or service?
- **How** do customers make choices?
- **When** will they buy the product or service?
- **Where** will they buy it?
- **Why** will they buy it?

If a business can answer these questions before it begins, then they will help it to be a success. The business will make smart decisions, and use its limited resources wisely.

But how does a business find the answers to these questions? By carrying out market research.

How to carry out market research

1 Decide on the information you require: that is, what questions you want answered. This will make sure you get the right information.

More later

2 Decide on the method to be employed in collecting this information.

3 Collect the information.

4 Interpret and use the information.

Collecting that information

Two kinds of information are available:

- primary data
- secondary data.

The second first

Secondary data is like second-hand information: somebody else has already done the leg-work. This readily available information can be used for your particular needs. It is information that already exists somewhere: for example, the Central Statistics Office provides information on the population; trade journals provide information on market trends. Other sources include libraries, Chambers of Commerce, Enterprise Ireland, etc.

Over to you

Can you suggest any other suitable sources of secondary data?

Primary Research

Sometimes the information you require may not be readily available, and so you may have to undertake *primary research* to secure first-hand information.

Undertaking your own market research: the options
1 Observation
Watch relevant people, actions, situations, etc. For example, check-out scanners at supermarkets provide first-hand information to the management on customers' preferences.

Over to you

Can you provide other examples of the collection of primary information using observation? Is it possible to observe everything?

2 Direct contact
Contact methods using direct contact with potential customers include interviews (individual and group) and questionnaires, through different channels—such as by telephone, by post, or in person.

If a business decides to undertake primary research, the method selected depends on needs, cost, and urgency.

Over to you

Rate the methods of collecting primary information by completing the following table:

	Information	Cost	Speed	Reliability
Telephone				
Post				
Personal contact				

★★★★★ = excellent   ★ = poor

In an ideal world, we could contact each of our customers and provide them with exactly what they need. In reality, of course, the best we can do is get a rough picture of what the typical customer would like, and attempt to satisfy them. A rough picture will be provided by studying a small *sample* of the total number of consumers, which will provide an impression of the bigger picture.

Selecting that sample

- Who is to be surveyed?
- How many people are to be surveyed (the sample size)?
- How are the people in the sample to be chosen (the sampling procedure)?

The information gathered from the research should help the business in deciding whether or not to proceed with the idea. Research avoids good money being thrown after a weak business project; it will also provide useful information when you are developing the *marketing mix*. In essence, it helps to focus the business on the road to success.

Go to Chapter 18

Get the connection!

At this stage you've got that idea for the product or service and, with luck, a good business name to go with it.

You now need to see whether you can sell the idea. To do this you should undertake some market research. The questionnaire is probably your best option.

Over to you

1 Decide

- Who will you interview?
- How many people will you interview? Obviously, the more people you interview the more information you will have.

Remember: *information is power* and will help your business to succeed.

2 Draw up a simple questionnaire

The information you need will dictate the questions to be asked.

Tips for compiling a questionnaire

Decisions to be made include:

- **what questions to ask**
- **the structure of the questions:**
    —closed questions: for example, those requiring 'Yes' or 'No' as an answer;
    —multiple-choice questions;
    —open-ended questions: giving the respondent the opportunity to air their views;

- **the wording of the questions:** this should be simple, direct, and concise;
- **the order of the questions:** the first question should arouse interest, while more difficult questions should come at the end. It is important not to bias the questions in favour of certain answers.

Your questionnaire should be easy to draw up if you keep in mind the information you seek. A good idea is to test the questionnaire first on your classmates.

Sample questionnaire

'Dressed for Dinner' proposed setting up a mini-enterprise to make and sell salad dressings. Before embarking on their business venture they decided to do some market research, and they compiled the following questionnaire.

Dressed for Dinner
A mini-enterprise producing salad dressings, mustards, and sauces

Questionnaire

Are you

☐ Male ☐ Female

☐ under 15? ☐ between 15 and 24? ☐ between 25 and 34?

☐ between 35 and 44? ☐ between 45 and 54? ☐ between 55 and 64?

☐ over 65?

Do you to prefer to buy produce that is made in Ireland?	Yes ☐ No ☐
Do you regularly buy produce that is made in Ireland?	Yes ☐ No ☐
Are you prepared to pay extra for Irish-made produce?	Yes ☐ No ☐
Are you employed in or in any way associated with the food industry?	Yes ☐ No ☐

If so, please state how. _____

Do you like salad dressings?	Yes ☐ No ☐

Which salad dressings do you like? _____

What brands do you usually buy? _____

Do you like mustard?	Yes ☐ No ☐

What brands do you usually buy? _____

Do you like sauces?	Yes ☐ No ☐

What sauces do you like? _____

What brands do you usually buy? _____

Thank you for taking the time to fill in this questionnaire.

Appropriate for postal questionnaire only!

3 Interpret and use the information

There's no use in collecting the information if you don't intend to use it. It should be read and interpreted with an open mind. Customers' responses can help to open your eyes and make you reassess the potential for success. This may result in abandoning your pet project ... but with luck it will be a case of short-term pain for long-term gain.

Go to page 90 for details

Now complete the *market research* part of your business plan.

CHAPTER FOURTEEN

The Blueprint: Prototype Development and Pricing

'A picture is worth a thousand words,' and so it is with a prototype. You've done the research, you believe you have a market; but before you invest thousands of pounds in a 'white elephant' it is a good idea to produce a finished sample of your proposed product—known as a **prototype**.

The prototype can be used to
- test the market for the proposed business
- show the viability of the proposed business to providers of finance
- take orders—your first sales
- cost the product
- set the selling price.

Getting the price right

The price is made up of two elements—the **cost** and the **profit**.
The cost is made up of three parts: *raw materials + labour + overheads*.

The raw materials

These can be classified as **direct** and **indirect**. Direct materials can be directly traced to a product: for example, when you produce a table, wood is obviously direct material. It could be said that direct materials are the main materials and are easily quantified and costed.

Indirect materials are necessary to produce a product but cannot be directly traced to the product, for example the glue used to stick the table together. It could be said that the indirect materials are minor materials, of insignificant quantity, and they are difficult to cost.

Over to you

Home Bakers is a group of four transition-year pupils. Allison, Rita, Billy and Seán have done market research that tells them that there would be a market for freshly baked scones at the eleven o'clock break in their school. They now want to test the market by producing some samples. Allison's father has given her the family recipe, which should make roughly twenty scones, as follows:

1 lb [450g] self-raising flour

4 oz [100g] butter

2 oz [50g] caster sugar

½ pint [300 ml] milk

A pinch of salt

1 Can you identify which raw materials are direct and which are indirect?

2 Billy, the purchasing manager, bought the ingredients in a local shop. Do you think Billy is a wise consumer? What advice would you give him when he is buying raw materials in future?

3 Billy has bought the following ingredients:

1 kg flour, 227 g butter, 1 litre milk

How much do you think each of these cost? (This will involve a trip to the shops.)

4 Home Bakers have asked their teacher how to work out the cost of the materials involved in making one batch of twenty scones. She started them off:

227g [½ lb] butter cost 85p …

but the recipe only requires 100 g. So, to calculate the exact cost of the butter used for this recipe, we do the following calculations:

$$227g = 85p \qquad\qquad 100g = \frac{85p}{227g} \times 100 = 37p$$

$$1g = \frac{85p}{227g} \qquad \text{(as required in recipe)}$$

Complete this procedure for the other ingredients.

5 Find the total cost of the raw materials.

6 This is the cost of the raw materials for twenty scones; find the cost of materials for one scone, i.e. the unit cost.

Labour

This can also be classified as direct or indirect.

Direct labour is the cost of employing the people who actually make the product. The usual rates of payment are by the hour (hourly rate) or by the number of units produced (piece rate).

Indirect labour costs include supervisors' and managers' pay. They don't produce any goods, but they have an important role to play in the production process. They are paid a set amount.

Over to you
Rita and Seán both like baking, and both got excellent results in Home Economics in the Junior Cert, so they are going to do the baking for the business. Suggest a method of payment for their labour. This must be added to the raw materials cost.

Note

It should take only ten to fifteen minutes to produce the raw scones: the oven does the rest of the work.

Overheads

These are the expenses incurred in a business that cannot be directly linked to the product or service: electricity, rent, telephone bill, stationery, and so on. These costs must be included when you are working out what to charge for the product or service.

Over to you

Can you name the overhead costs Home Bakers are likely to incur? Remember:

Raw materials + Labour + Overheads = Cost of the product

We've worked out the cost … now what price do we charge?

1   What is the lowest price a business should charge for its product or service?
2   Is the sky the limit when you are deciding how high the price can be? (Consider the customer's perception of the value of the product.)

Some pricing approaches

1 Cost-plus pricing

Having worked out the cost of the product or service, the business can add on a figure for profit. If it decides to add 10 per cent to the cost, this will represent pure profit and is called the *mark-up*.

Can you identify the advantages and the disadvantages of using this pricing method?

2 Break-even pricing or target pricing

Using this method, the business tries to work out the price at which it will cover all costs but without making a profit (that is, at which it will *break even*). Alternatively, it can choose a profit so as to set the price—*target pricing*.

A *break-even chart* can be used in break-even pricing. This is a simple line graph in which total sales revenue is plotted against total cost at various levels of sales (also called *sales volume*). Where the two lines cross is the *break-even point*.

$$Total\ sales\ revenue = Selling\ price \times Quantity\ sold$$

$$Total\ cost = Fixed\ costs + Variable\ costs$$

Up to a certain point—a certain level of output—fixed costs do not change as output changes. Examples include rent, insurance, and telephone bills.

Over to you
Can you think of other examples of fixed costs?

Fruit Fayre Ltd ... A Case Study

Fixed costs

Fruit Fayre Ltd are thinking of producing a range of jams, jellies, and chutneys. The firm decides to rent a premises, and, having shopped around, they have chosen one that gives them the capacity to produce 20,000 jars. The rent on this premises is a fixed cost: it must be paid whether they produce and sell 20,000 jars or none at all. However, if they decided to produce 30,000 jars they would need a bigger premises, and so the rent would change.

Variable costs

Variable costs change as output changes. The more you produce, the greater the variable costs. Examples include raw materials and direct labour.

Can you think of examples of other variable costs?

Back to Fruit Fayre ...
Having done some research, this company believes it can sell its products for £2 a jar. The fixed costs for the year will be £10,000, and the variable cost is £1.20 a jar. How many jars will the company need to sell to break even, that is, to cover al its costs without making a profit?

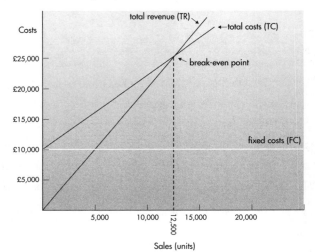

Take a look at the following break-even chart:

We can see from the graph that total revenue and total costs are equal at 12,500 jars. This is the break-even point.

To simplify this, we have a formula for calculating the break-even point:

$$\frac{Fixed\ costs}{Selling\ price\ per\ unit - Variable\ cost\ per\ unit}$$

i.e.

$$\frac{10,000}{2 - 1.20} = \frac{10,000}{0.80} = 12,500\ jars$$

Maths check

Sales revenue (12,500 jars × £2):   25,000

Variable costs (12,500 jars × £1·20):   15,000

                                          10,000

Fixed costs: 10,000

Profit   ————

If Fruit Fayre wishes to sell its products at £2 a jar it will have to sell 12,500 jars to break even. If the business plans to make a profit of £5,000, then it would have to sell 18,750 jars.

How do I know this?

Fruit Fayre calculated that a return (or profit) of £5,000 on their investment was a realistic and necessary target profit for the viability of the project (as stated in their business plan). This target profit of £5,000 could be considered another 'cost' on the business, as it must be covered for the business to continue. Therefore, this profit is similar to a fixed cost.

Applying our formula again,

$$\frac{Fixed\ costs + Target\ profit}{Selling\ price\ per\ unit - Variable\ costs\ per\ unit}$$

$$\frac{10,000 + 5,000}{2 - 1.20} = \frac{15,000}{0.80} = 18,750\ jars$$

Fruit Fayre can undertake cost volume profit (CVP) analysis (which is based on break-even pricing) to estimate how changes in

—variable cost per unit,

—sales price,

—fixed costs and

—sales volume

would affect profit before the business finally decides what price to charge for its products.

3 Value-based pricing

This method uses the buyer's perception of value—not the cost of making the product—as the key to setting the selling price. This price then dictates decisions regarding the design and costs of the product.

Over to you

1 What are the advantages of using this pricing approach?

2 Can you see any difficulty a business might encounter when using this approach?

Get the connection!

Guidelines for making prototypes

1 When you are making your samples, bear in mind the following guidelines:

- The prototype must be perfect.
- It must be an exact replica of what you propose to sell when you have established your business.
- Don't forget to cost it.

2 Having made the prototype, use it in carrying out further market research. Draw up a questionnaire to find out answers to such questions as:

- Are your potential customers still interested in the product or service on offer?
- What price would they be prepared to pay for it?
- Could they make any suggestions about how the product could be improved?

3 You have several costing options; perhaps the most straightforward is cost-plus pricing. Don't forget to include the cost of

—phone calls

—stationery

—postage

—packaging etc.

CHAPTER FIFTEEN

Finding Finance for Business

In a simple world, a businessperson would use private funds to invest in the business, thereby allowing them complete control over the growth and direction of the enterprise. Some people are fortunate in that they can use a redundancy payment, their life assurance policy or even a lottery win to finance a business idea. However, few people are wealthy enough to go it on their own. There is a need, therefore, to tap in to other sources of finance.

A business requires finance

- at start-up
- when expanding, and
- from day to day.

> 'We haven't got the money, so we've got to think.'
> —Lord Rutherford

Start-up finance

A basic rule for financing a new business is: 'As little as possible, as cheaply as possible.'

There are essentially only two types of finance:

- *equity*—money (capital) invested in the business by the owners or shareholders
- *debt*—money (capital) lent to the business.

Equity or ownership finance

The owner's investment is usually the initial money spent in the business. The owner shoulders the risk of losing all should the business fail. If you are not able to provide all the required finance yourself, it may be necessary to raise outside finance. New equity capital is normally raised from people who are prepared to take the risks associated with new ventures in the hope that they can share in the reward when the business succeeds. Buying shares in a company makes you a *shareholder* or part-owner of the business.

Raising capital through shares: how does it work?

If the business is a limited company, the owners invest capital by buying shares. Being a shareholder gives you the right to a say in how the company is run (though you might not be involved in the day-to-day running of the business). A shareholder receives a **share certificate** to prove their part ownership of the company, and a shareholders' meeting is held at least annually.

Shareholders have an opportunity to share in any profits that are made. Any profit left over after tax and interest has been paid will, if the directors agree, be divided up among the shareholders as **dividends**. If later you decide to 'sell up' as a shareholder in the company, you can sell your shareholding on to another investor—hopefully at a profit.

Over to you

It is not always easy to divest youself of your shareholding in a company. Can you think of companies that might be experiencing difficulty attracting new shareholders at the present time? Other companies have queues of investors screaming to buy their shares; can you name any of these businesses?

Debt, or borrowed finance

Debt comes in a variety of forms, from a simple loan from a friend, with the condition that it be paid back by next Saturday, to overdrafts, term loans, long-term loans, and mortgages. Financial institutions that provide **debentures** or loan capital to companies are known as **debenture-holders**, and the interest on the debenture must be paid every year. Because you have to pay interest on debt, you should try to manage with as little as possible.

Not over yet: survival of the fittest!

One of the most important factors for success in business is planning. Despite what you might think, entrepreneurs who are consistently successful are not *extravagant* risk-takers but rather prefer to undertake 'calculated' risks. Financial planning is one area of the business plan that is crucial to the survival and development of the enterprise.

The finance section of the business plan

Most readers of business plans have a vested interest. They are preparing to invest in your business or to lend money to the business: therefore they will pay special attention to the finance section. Finance projections are an important aspect of this section, including final accounts and cash flow forecasts. Financial projections must be able to withstand questioning, as few people will invest or lend money if it's not in capable hands.

The question of cash: Think cash, cash, cash

Getting your start-up finance is one hurdle; keeping the company in good financial health is another. You need to know when money is coming in, and when it is going out. The cash is the lifeblood of the business and should be monitored rigorously. Many companies can be profitable on paper but can fail because of lack of cash. For example, the business may have achieved record sales, but if half these sales are on credit and payment has yet to be received, the profitable company may die of cash starvation.

Cash budgeting for a business

Preparing a cash flow forecast

The following cash flow forecast shows a business that began with £10,000 capital—£8,000 from the owner, £2,000 on loan. The owner has calculated how much cash is likely to come in over the first six months, from her capital together with cash from sales. It represents an estimate of what the business will be 'earning' from month to month. Listed underneath these are all the outgoings of the business, including wages, purchases of materials, and electricity.

The forecast looks detailed, but it is a very useful way of planning what the cash needs of the business will be. For example, the owner now knows that there will be a shortage of £600 in April and can plan to remedy this or find the most appropriate and cost-effective source of finance for this. A cash flow forecast is similar to a household budget where monthly finances are planned.

Cash flow forecast for Starship Enterprises

		Jan.	Feb.	Mar.	Apr.	May.	Jun.
	Receipts						
	Cash sales	—	5,000	4,000	2,000	2,000	2,000
	Debtors (credit sales)	—	—	2,000	3,000	6,000	7,000
	Loan	2,000	—	—	—	—	—
	Owner's capital	8,000	—	—	—	—	—
(A)	**Total receipts**	10,000	5,000	6,000	5,000	8,000	9,000
	Payments						
	Purchases	5,000	3,000	5,000	6,000	4,000	3,000
	Wages	1,000	1,000	1,000	2,000	2,000	2,000
	Rent	500	500	500	500	500	500
	Electricity	—	600	—	—	650	—
(B)	**Total payments**	6,500	5,100	6,500	8,500	7,150	5,500
(A – B)	Net cash at end of month	3,500	(100)	(500)	(3,500)	850	3,500
	Opening cash	—	3,500	3,400	2,900	(600)	250
	Closing cash	3,500	3,400	2,900	(600)	250	(3,750)

You're in business—now for survival

A business, like a household, will have day-to-day *current* costs as well as long-term *capital* costs.

Over to you

From the following list, identify which are current expenses and which are capital costs:

Purchase of premises

Electricity bills

Leasing of van

Gas bill

Purchase of computers

Can you think of a few more examples of current and capital expenditure for a typical business?

We are aware of what the business spends its money on; but where does it get this money? Stick to the basic financial management rule: match the need to the source.

For example, buying premises is a long-term requirement, and it should be matched with a long-term source. Therefore, a long-term loan is the suitable source of finance—unless you can see clearly that you will have enough money within a short space of time to repay it. Taking out a short-term loan or an overdraft to buy premises is a recipe for disaster. You will have to renegotiate the loan with the bank time and again—and if your business runs into temporary difficulties, you run the risk of losing everything if the bank calls in the loan.

Over to you

Can you think of other reasons why this is an ill-advised financial arrangement?

Short-term loans, or even overdrafts, are more suited to financing stock or debtors, because you should be able to repay the loan once you have sold the goods or got the money in.

In summary: sources of finance for the business

Over to you

Matching sources with uses.

Short-term sources	Used to finance
Accrued expenses	Telephone, electricity, etc.
Bank overdraft	
rade credit	
Factoring debts	

Medium-term sources	Used to finance
Term loan	
Hire-purchase	
Leasing	

Long-term sources	Used to finance
Capital (both equity and debt)	
Long-term loan (debenture)	
Retained earnings (i.e. profits ploughed back in to the business)	

Advise Jack and Jill ...

Jack and Jill have set up a bakery. They need to buy extra raw materials for the forthcoming festival weekend but are short of cash. They have asked your advice on a suitable source of finance; what do you suggest?

As this is a short-term requirement, I would suggest 'leaning' on their trade credit: that is, buying their raw materials through their creditors, and paying for these goods when the cash situation improves.

Opening a business bank account

Opening a business bank account is similar to opening an ordinary bank account, with some exceptions.

The business must provide the necessary legal documents drawn up on the formation of the company; and the authorised signatories for the bank account must be appointed.

Over to you

1 Which type of bank account will the company open, current account or deposit account? Why?

2 Identify the bank services the business might use that a household might also use.

3 Identify services used mainly by the bank's business customers (for example, night safe facilities).

Have you any other ideas?

Get the connection!

1 Decide how much money you need to kick-start your business. Always plan for unforeseen expenditure!

2 Where will your mini-enterprise secure start-up finance? Here are some suggestions:
- Sell shares.
- Take out a loan.
- Each class member or director contributes money to the business, receiving an IOU from the finance department.
- Organise money-raising activities that require little or no capital to set up.

3 Can you prepare a cash flow forecast for your business?

Memorandum

To: Directors

From: Finance director

Re: Raising finance

Date: 10 Sep. 1999

There seems to be some confusion about this issue. Please keep in mind the following points when making the final decision:

1. How much is realistically required to get the first project off the ground?

2. What do you intend to do with the money?

3. How long do you need it for?

---

4 Now complete the *finance* part of your business plan.

Go to page 90

CHAPTER SIXTEEN

Organising the Business

There are many different types of business. All these businesses are organised in accordance with structures laid down by the law. As businesses grow and develop, the form of legal organisation that suits their activities may change.

Business structures are divided into the following groups:

- *sole traders*—one-person businesses
- *partnerships*—owned and controlled by more than one person
- *limited liability companies*—private limited companies (Ltd) and public limited companies (PLC)
- *co-operatives*—owned by the people who work in them (producer co-operatives or worker co-operatives) or by the customers who buy from them (retail co-operatives)
- *state-owned companies*—owned by the state on behalf of the general public.

Over to you

Can you give examples of each of the business structures described above?

Most businesses are structured as sole traders, partnerships, or limited liability companies.

A sole trader: J. J. Maguire, plumbing engineer

Sole trader

J.J. Maguire started out working for herself as a plumber five years ago. Having saved to provide for the start-up capital, she advertised in the Golden Pages, and hasn't been short of work since. She likes working for herself, deciding her own working hours, and keeping the profits for herself. She is subject to certain pressures, mainly if the business loses money: then her personal belongings are at risk, because she has 'unlimited liability'. Working in isolation, and the difficulty of obtaining extra capital for expansion, are other possible problems.

Partnership

J.J. can solve a number of the problems she faces by forming a **partnership**. She has decided to go into partnership with a friend, Seán Graham. Seán has experience in installing central heating; he is also willing to put £5,000 into the business. Since they formed the partnership, new ideas and different approaches are coming to the surface, and each partner can specialise in their own field.

Believing he is the fount of all knowledge, Seán has the annoying habit of making decisions on behalf of the partnership without consulting J.J. Decisions made by one partner can be binding on the other; and disagreements could lead to the break-up of the partnership.

Over to you

Can you advise Seán and J.J. on any other difficulties they might encounter? Advise them on how they might resolve conflicts in the course of their business.

Limited liability

Unlimited and limited liability—the difference could mean everything.

Limited company

Unlimited liability means that if the business cannot pay its creditors (the people or firms to whom it owes money), the owners may be declared bankrupt. If this happens, the owners' personal possessions, including their homes, could be taken and used to pay for the debts of the business.

Limited liability means that the owners' (i.e. shareholders') responsibilities for the debts of the company are limited to the amount they have invested in the company. For example, if the company goes into liquidation a shareholder with £100 of shares could lose only the £100, and not any of their personal possessions. The benefit of this is that potential shareholders will not be put off investing by the possibility of losing everything they own.

I want the protection of limited liability. How do I go about it?

A sole trader or partnership may wish to remove the risk of unlimited liability by forming a *private limited company*.

Private limited company (Ltd)

J.J. and Seán have decided to take this course and are going to form a company, which they will call Oakpark Plumbing and Heating Engineers Ltd. As a limited company it will have its own legal personality, separate from that of its owners. Other family members have decided to invest in the business, thereby becoming shareholders or part-owners of the business; they will obtain shares that entitle them to a share of the profits in proportion to the number of shares they own.

Do you remember the name we give to the share of profit the shareholder receives?

Certain restrictions are placed on private limited companies. The shares cannot be sold to the public (for example through the Stock Exchange), so they have to be sold privately, and with the agreement of the existing shareholders.

Going public

The shares in a public limited company can be sold to members of the public. The shareholders then become part-owners of the company and have certain rights:

1 to receive the company's annual reports, including accounts;
2 to attend, speak and vote at the company's annual general meeting (AGM);
3 to elect the board of directors and the chairman of the board.

As many PLCs have their shares traded on the Stock Exchange, the shareholder can sell the shares (now 'second-hand') to anyone who is willing to buy them. It is possible that shares could be bought in this way by companies intent on a take-over bid. Other drawbacks include the legal requirement to publish full annual accounts, lengthy and costly set-up procedures, and the possibility of communication problems between the management and the work force as the company grows.

Over to you
Complete the following table

	Advantages	Disadvantages
Sole trader		
Partnership		
Co-operative		
Private limited company		
Public limited company		

The traditional organisational family tree of a large limited company

shareholders (owners)

↓ *elect*

directors (senior management)

↓ *appoint*

managing director (day-to-day manager)

↓

managers (middle management)

↓

employees

The owners of limited companies are the shareholders, who entrust the control of limited companies to the board of directors they have elected.

What do managers really do?

Some people have an impression that managers do little but earn lots of money, on the back of other people's work. However, an effective manager holds a highly responsible position and has more than enough work on his or her shoulders if the business is to succeed. An effective manager will be responsible for the following activities:

Planning

Strategic planning is one of the most crucial management functions. Decisions such as where to establish a factory, the products to be manufactured and how resources should be employed are all keys to the company's growth. The more skilled the management is in planning, the more successful the company is likely to be.

Organising

This refers to the smooth running of the company: that departments are aware of each other's activities and of the decisions taken, so that there is no duplication, friction, or lack of understanding.

Controlling

Once the plans for the company have been established, effective management ensures that the objectives are achieved. They compare the plan with actual results; where they diverge greatly, the management needs to investigate the reasons for these differences and report back to the next planning meeting.

Who does what?

Most groups, if left to their own devices, will naturally settle into their own niche, organising activities that engage their interests and talents. Organisations big and small divide the work to be done along distinct lines, or departments.

Each department of a company has its own functions and responsibilities, presided over by a department manager answerable to the managing director, board of directors, and, ultimately, shareholders.

Many businesses are structured along the following departmental lines:

Sales and Marketing

One of its functions is to form a link between the company and the customer, usually through a network of sales representatives, and to make sure that sales targets are reached. It is also responsible for market research and product policy, helping to produce the right product at the right price.

Production

This department is responsible for changing the raw materials into the finished product. This department organises a production schedule to make sure that adequate supplies of the product are on hand at all times. The manager must take into account the type of factory and machinery they have at their disposal and the level of skilled labour they require.

Purchasing

The purchasing manager is responsible for buying the raw materials and anything else the company needs—everything from production machinery to office supplies.

Personnel or Human Resources

The aim is to recruit the right people for the firm's departments and to help them to settle in to the company.

Finance

This department monitors the inflow and outflow of payments and deals with all the monetary aspects of the company.

Get the connection

utting the best team in place

There are two approaches that can be taken in a classroom situation:

1 **The interview approach.** Each member of the mini-enterprise applies for a position in the business, by completing an application form or submitting a CV. Candidates are interviewed by a panel, perhaps the principal, a teacher, or an outside businessperson, and the most suitable person is selected for each position.

2 **The 'general election' approach.** Pupils decide on the position they are interested in undertaking, and justify in front of the class why they are the best person for the job. It is ultimately the class group that democratically elects the person to do the job.

Reality check

The most popular pupil is not necessarily the most effective one to do the job! If the job is not done properly during the term, you can lose the job.

Rewarding the team

Payment can be a problem! Different approaches can be taken, including:

1 **Payment by the hour.** Set a rate per hour, and the team get paid for hours spent on work relating to the mini-enterprise.

How do you keep track of the hours worked by the whole team? Using a simple and easy-to-operate system, the personnel manager arranges that each team member receives a *time card*. It is up to each member

Name:		Job description	
Date	Hours worked		Initials

- to keep an accurate record of their work and
- to make sure the time card is stamped or initialled by the personnel manager each week or each month. The personnel manager must make sure the time

card is an accurate record of the time invested by each member in the business. Payment is based on the hours accrued on the time card and will be made at agreed intervals during the life-span of the business.

This self-policing payment system allows each team member transparency in relation to work and payment matters.

Over to you

Can you suggest hourly rates for the general manager, department managers, and staff?

2 Payment per unit. This is an alternative method, where each member of the team is paid according to the number of units produced. Depending on the production target set for the week, each member of the production team is allocated a personal production target; bonus payments could be made to those members who exceed their target. A production card could be used, similar to a time card. A word of caution: keep product quality in mind at all times.

3 Payment by commission. Commission is a percentage of sales income. The more you sell, the more you get paid!

4 Payment on winding up. With this system, payment is decided when you are winding up the business. The money that is left over on liquidation (after all debts have been paid off) can be used to pay the team members. It can be divided equally or according to participation in the business.

The gold star reward system

This system can be used in conjunction with any of the other payment methods. It gives recognition and reward to those members of the team who have gone that extra mile. Essentially, it rewards hard work.

Mini-enterprise members can be nominated weekly or monthly by fellow-members for a gold star award. The team should decide what form the gold star award should take.

CHAPTER SEVENTEEN

Producing the Goods

Having decided on the product to produce, the business can set a sales target. This target helps them to plan the quantity to produce.

The methods of production

The next decision is *how* to produce. Three main options are available to a business when deciding how to produce: these are called the **production processes**. We will now take a look at each.

Job production

This production process is appropriate whenever a business has to produce individual items to special requirements. Goods are made to order and are unique products, or originals. Examples include a ship, haute couture clothing, or a bridge.

Mass production

Most of us are familiar with the long production lines that produce everything from television sets to tinned peas and from cars to soft drinks. The idea of mass production is to make a very large number of identical products as cheaply as possible.

An aspect of this method of production is that it is very machine-intensive (*capital-intensive*). This production process requires strict planning, as unplanned interruptions in the production process cost money.

Batch production

This third production technique falls somewhere between the first two. Any product that needs to be made in reasonably large but limited numbers is usually made using the batch production approach. Examples include the manufacture of different styles of shoes, or print runs of different books in a printing company.

Over to you

Can you give examples of other products suited to the different production processes?

Modern developments in production

In recent times, new trends have emerged in the area of production. These radical changes have been driven by technology.

Computer-aided design

With the assistance of a CAD program, designers can design products and experiment with changes to the product without the need for hundreds of detailed technical drawings.

Computer-aided manufacturing

Parts of the production process are controlled by one or more computers. These computers do many of the tasks that aid manufacturing and that would have taken human beings many hours in the past, such as setting the production plan, timetabling the machines required, and so on.

Computer-integrated manufacturing

CIM allows the whole production process to be regulated by a computer system. Such a system can spot problems, communicate them to other computers integrated in the production process, and remedy the problem quickly.

Just-in-time production

Originating in Japan, JIT production aims to eliminate waste in every form and at every level, and thus reduce costs. The purchase and storage of stock (raw materials, partly finished goods, and finished goods) has always been a drain on the financial resources of most enterprises. Promoters of the JIT principle would take some of the following steps to reduce this burden:

- Make sure stock is delivered just in time to be used in the production line. This reduces storage costs, the risk of obsolescence, the risk of theft, etc.
- Suppliers are hand-picked to provide the exact raw materials for the business.
- Demand for the finished product dictates production—a 'demand pull' system rather than the traditional 'supply push' system.

Over to you

The high standards demanded by the JIT system have implications throughout the entire business. Can you identify some of these implications?

Total quality management

Quality refers to the ability of the product to do its job. However, the Japanese take the concept of quality further—TQM. This is an effort to constantly improve quality in every part of the business. It requires total dedication to continuous quality improvement and preventing defects before they occur. It aims to improve customer value and can be a powerful weapon in achieving 'total customer satisfaction'.

These represent some of the important trends in business in recent times. Others include the move towards 'outsourcing' (contracting out certain business activities, e.g. production, advertising, etc.) and the 'world-class business' (WCB) model (to be the best in every aspect of the business).

Setting your business apart!

To survive in business it is necessary to be the best that you can be. This entails doing that little bit extra. One way in which a business can secure an advantage is by focusing on the intangible aspects of the business, in particular on quality. Quality can differentiate you from your competitors; and because it is an intangible factor it is also more difficult to copy. In the highly competitive grocery trade, where it is difficult to distinguish a somewhat standard service, one supermarket chain has adopted an approach that it claims is different from that of its competitors: quality in all areas, based on the principle that the customer is king (or queen).

Some businesses pursuing quality can even gain recognition for it in the form of awards, such as the internationally recognised ISO 9000 award or the Q mark.

Quality can sometimes be the ultimate distinguishing factor in the eyes of the customer, particularly in service industries. Some enterprises make quality the backbone of their business by pursuing TQM.

Keeping one step ahead

Some businesses are victims of their own success: they fail to update and adapt their original successful idea to the increasing demands of customers and the modern business environment. It is important to be aware of customers' changing expectations and desires and to undertake research and development (R&D) for your product accordingly. R&D takes a variety of forms, from basic customer surveys to expensive high-tech experimental projects.

Get the connection!

The research is done, the product or service has been selected; now you're ready to go!

1 You've worked out how many units you need to make and sell to break even. From their product costings, the finance team should be able to provide these figures.

2 From your market research, perhaps you can sell more than you require to break even and so make a profit.

3 Based on the calculated break-even for your business and projected sales, it is now up to the management team to set a realistic production target.

4 Consider the following important factors:

The time available for production

'Sure they're queuing up for our tie-dyed T-shirts; of course we'll get around to making them.' All very well, but when?

Count the number of weeks your mini-enterprise will be in existence; don't forget to allow for planned, and unplanned, disturbances to the normal routine.

Count the number of hours (classes) that can be allocated to production each week; time should be allowed for meetings (planning and feedback) and administration.

Staffing levels

Keep in mind the number of workers available, allowing for absenteeism. Have they the necessary skills?

Raw materials

Remember to buy raw materials at the right price, in the right quantity and quality, at the right time.

It may be necessary to appoint a purchasing manager to complete this job, as it is a vital link in the whole process.

Remember that the JIT principle can apply just as effectively to your mini-enterprise as to a large multinational company.

Recording production

The following sample record of production should help you to keep tight control over the production process.

Date: _____

Time spent on production: _____

Names of production team: _____

Number of items completed: _____

Number of items started but not finished: _____

Number of items unsuitable for sale: _____

Reasons: _____

Other problems during this production run: _____

Comments: _____

Signed: [production manager] _____

Storage

It is important to store your raw materials and finished goods safely and securely. There are several risks to be considered: the risk of theft, of obsolescence, perishability, etc.

Memorandum

To: The Production Team

From: Words of Wisdom Consultants

Re: Production Tips

1. Choose an efficient method of production.
2. Be cost-effective.
3. Keep waste to a minimum.
4. Quality should not be sacrificed in the name of cost.
5. Be market-driven, not product-driven.
6. Prepare for all eventualities.

Now complete the production section of your business plan.

'Give them quality. That's the best kind of advertising.'
—Milton Hershey

CHAPTER EIGHTEEN

Selling the Goods

'A man without a smiling face must not open a shop.'
—Chinese proverb

The customer is at the heart of the marketing process. A market can be divided into segments, and a business should select the segments at which it wishes to aim its product or service—the target market.

When selecting a segment of the market, a business should keep in mind its competitors and should aim to sell to those segments where it has a competitive advantage. Finding a competitive advantage could be the key to winning and keeping customers. A business should aim to understand the needs and buying processes of its customers better than competitors do and try to deliver more value.

USP

If a business can find its **unique selling point** (USP) and promote that aspect that differentiates it from other products, this will set it apart from the competition and, hopefully, boost sales.

Identifying possible competitive advantages will help a business in positioning its product in the market.

Over to you

There are many businesses in the retail grocery market. How do they differentiate themselves from their competitors?

The next stage is to design a marketing mix, in order to position the product in the selected target segment.

The marketing mix

There are five ingredients in the marketing mix—the five Ps:

The five Ps

- product
- price
- place
- promotion
- packaging

The product: what the customer wants

P1

28 per cent of all ideas for new products come from watching and listening to customers: market research is a continuing process. A business must not only develop new products but must also manage the product as it goes through its life-cycle.

The product life-cycle

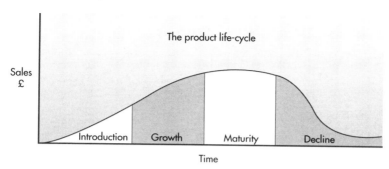

Introduction

The product or service is introduced to the market. Sales can be slow as the customer is introduced to the new product, and profits are low, as money has to be used to push the product.

Growth

If the product survives the introduction stage it enters the next phase, where sales and profit grow steadily. Competitors may enter at this stage, so a business may have to fight back to hold on to its market share by, for example, improving quality, adding new features, or entering new market segments.

Over to you

Can you suggest other ways of fighting back?

Maturity

Sales growth slows down, and profits stabilise. This stage lasts longer than previous stages. As a defence tactic, competitors that are vigorously defending their share of this mature market may cut prices. A business has several options in this case:

- to improve features of the product (perhaps by investing in R&D)
- to try to attract new customers
- to match the price reductions of competitors (though this may cause a futile price war)
- to launch an aggressive sales campaign.

Decline

Sales start to fall off, and so profits decline. This may happen because of

- changes in technology (as happened with the typewriter and the record-player)
- shifts in consumers' tastes
- saturation of the market by competitors.

Products and services pass through the various stages of the life-cycle but at different speeds. This should be viewed as a challenge and faced head on by

● finding new products to replace aging ones
● understanding how products age, and adapting your marketing strategy accordingly.

Over to you

Can you identify products at the various stages of the life-cycle? Can you think of any products that have raced through the product life-cycle: here today, gone tomorrow?

Branding

The customer sees the brand as an important part of the product or service. A brand can help set a business apart. Developing a brand costs time and money, but if successfully developed it can be very powerful.

A brand is more than a name: it can include a symbol, a sign, or a design.

Can you identify any brands? Are there any differences between branded and unbranded goods? Are you a slave to 'sought-after' brands?

The price: the cost to the customer

P2

There is no such thing as a free lunch, and everything has its price. When setting prices, a business should consider the following:

1 **Marketing objectives.** These can include survival, maximising profit or market share, being the product quality leader, etc.

Can you think of any other marketing objectives?

2 **Marketing mix strategy.** The other four Ps will affect the price selected by the business to charge for its product.
3 **Costs.** These set the floor price that a business can charge for its product or service.

Over to you

1 What are the costs that must be covered?
2 Costs can be classified into two main categories. Name them.
3 Do costs remain the same regardless of the level of production?

The three factors described above are considered to be internal (within the business's own control). But that isn't the full picture, as there are external factors also to be considered.

4 **The demand for the product.** If the business sets the price too high, then the demand will be adversely affected.

Over to you

Can you name other factors a business cannot control that will adversely affect demand?

5 **Competitors' prices or special offers.** It is important for a business to benchmark its price against its competitors.

6 **Economic conditions.** These have a strong impact on price.

Do you think people are likely to spend more during a boom or during a recession? Why?

7 **Government policy.** The Government monitors prices and has the power to affect pricing decisions.

8 **Social and environmental concerns.** These also have to be considered.

Which type of petrol is cheaper, leaded or unleaded? Why?

Pricing products: the strategies

1 **Premium pricing strategy.** This may be pursued if the product is of high quality and the customer is prepared to pay a high price.

2 **Economy pricing strategy.** This is the reverse of premium pricing: a lower price is charged, but the product may also be of a lower quality.

3 **Market penetration pricing.** At first a low price is set to penetrate the market quickly. It is hoped that a large number of customers will be attracted and the business will win a large market share. High sales will then enable the business to maintain its low price.

4 **Discount pricing.** This involves giving price reductions if goods are bought in large quantities, or for cash, or out of season.

5 **Segmented pricing.** Different customers are charged different prices, for example reduced prices to the cinema and theatre for children, students, or pensioners.

Over to you

Can you think of other examples of segmented pricing?

6 **Psychological pricing.** The price can often say something about a product, and customers often feel that price equals quality—that the higher the price, the higher the quality.

Another form of psychological pricing is the 95p illusion. For example, an electrical shop displays a television set with a price tag of £299.95, rather than £300. It seems cheaper, doesn't it? Some customers will even view it as nearer to £200 than £300 and proceed to make the 'bargain purchase'.

Do you think psychological pricing works?

Pricing is a dynamic process, and a business often has to adjust its prices to account for different customers and as a product passes through its life-cycle.

Place: convenience for the customer

P3

How to get the product or service from the producer to the customer is what is meant by the term 'place'. A business can sell directly to the customer or may go through intermediaries—wholesalers and retailers. These are known as the *channels of distribution*.

Wholesalers buy the goods from the manufacturers and in turn sell to the retailers, who sell to us, the customers. Selecting the correct channel of distribution is important, as it has an effect on the other variables in the marketing mix. It also determines how well the target customers gain access to the product or service.

We are all familiar with the traditional distribution channel:

Producer
↓
Wholesaler
↓
Retailer
↓
Customer

But in recent years the **vertical marketing system** has developed. It consists of producers, wholesalers and retailers working together. One channel member owns the others and so dominates. Examples include oil companies that own petrol stations, and breweries that own pubs.

Over to you

Can you think of any others?

Promotion: communication with the customer

The main tools available for promoting a product or service are:

- advertising
- sales promotion
- public relations
- personal selling.

P4

It is important to aim the promotion campaign at the correct market segment, i.e. those customers you wish to attract. The next hurdle is choosing a message. The message should get **attention**, hold **interest**, arouse **desire**, and obtain **action**. Content and structure are important when designing the message for the campaign.

AIDA

Advertising

1 Where can a business advertise its product or service?

2 'Surveys show that people do not trust advertising claims.' Discuss this statement.

Sales promotion

Sales promotion covers a wide range of short-term incentives to boost sales, including money-off coupons, 'buy one, get one free,' 25 per cent extra, competitions, etc. Can you come up with other examples?

Public relations

Public relations means trying to get publicity and promoting a positive image of the business by means of press statements, product launches, etc. Increasingly, sponsorship is being employed as a form of PR to enhance the image of the business.

'Doing business without advertising is like winking at a girl across a darkened room: you know what you are doing, but no-one else does.'

—Anonymous

Personal selling

Personal selling explains itself, and consists of the people who actually sell the product or service.

Over to you

Identify a good and a bad advertisement. What makes a good advertisement good, in your opinion?

P5

Packaging: first impressions

The product's packaging communicates to the customer its design, shape, colour, and purpose.

The primary function of packaging is the protection of the product; but the following issues should also be considered:

- whether childproof
- whether tamper-resistant
- the size, shape, materials used, and colour
- environmental issues.

Food for thought

The average supermarket stocks between 15,000 and 17,000 products. The average shopper passes by 300 items a minute; and 53 per cent of purchases are made on impulse.

1 Can you give three examples of products you believe have good packaging? Why is the packaging good, in your opinion?

2 Can you give three examples of innovative packaging?

Get the connection!

Many large businesses have lots of money to spend developing the marketing mix. Though the resources in your mini-enterprise are limited, it is still important to consider the five Ps.

The product

- Can you sell it? Consider design, colour, shape, weight.
- Can you make it to a high standard?

Price

- How will you decide on the price to charge?
- Don't forget you must be able to cover your costs—but don't be greedy! If you set too high a price, nobody will buy, no matter how good the product.

Place

- Where are you going to sell your product?
- Don't rely solely on family, friends, classmates, or teachers (the sympathy vote!).
- Try to find retail outlets: you may be self-employed next summer rather than looking for a job.

Promotion

- Where can you advertise your product or service?
- How can you advertise it?
- Can you devise a sales promotion campaign to launch your business?
- Get a good sales team together to sell the product.
- Most schools provide you with a captive audience. Use it!

Now complete the *marketing* section of your business plan.

Go to page 90

Assignment

1 List what you consider to be five luxury products or services and five necessities.
  (a) Make a list of words that describe how you feel about each.
  (b) Are there differences between the words you use to describe the luxuries and the necessities? (Advertisers are aware of these differences and use emotive language when devising campaigns.)

2 Think of a purchase that you made recently.
  (a) Were you aware that your friends had a similar product or service?
  (b) Did this influence your purchase decision? Why, or why not?

3 Look at advertisements on television or in magazines, or listen to advertisements on the radio. Select five; can you identify who they are aimed at, i.e. the target market?

4 Make a list of five items that appear to be new products the next time you visit a supermarket. Rate them from ★ to ★★★★★, using innovation as your criterion.

5 Choose a personal care product (including cosmetics) that you use regularly.

(a) How much does it cost?

(b) Why do you use this product?

(c) Are there benefits communicated through the price?

(d) Does the price suggest good value?

(e) Do you think you are being overcharged, or undercharged? Why, or why not?

6 Survey the petrol prices in your locality. Note (a) the brand, (b) the price per litre of leaded and unleaded, (c) the distance to the nearest competitor, and (d) the prices charged by competitors. What conclusions can you draw from your research?

CHAPTER NINETEEN

Keeping Accounts

Keeping accounts is something we do every day, though we might not always be aware of it. We keep account of our homework in our notebook, and we keep track of the money in our pocket. Businesses must keep detailed records—*accounts*—to keep them on the right track.

The word 'account' in everyday language is often used to mean an explanation or a report of certain actions or events. In a basic way, we have always been involved in some form of accounting. It may have gone no further than a farmer measuring his worth simply by counting the number of cows or sheep that he owned.

Accounting for a farmer's wealth

His possessions	A year ago	Now	Change
Cows	●●●●●●●●●●	●●●●●●●●●●●●●●●●	
Hens (● = 10)	●●●●●●●●●●	●●●●●●●	
Pigs	●●●●●	●●●●	
Sheep (● = 10)	●●●●●	●●●●●●●	
Land (● = 1 acre)	●●●●	●●●●	
Cottage	●	●	
Carts	●●●	●	
Ploughs	●	●●	

Over to you

1 Complete the change column in the table above.

2 Can you predict any difficulties that might arise with the above system of recording-keeping?

The table on the previous page illustrates just how difficult it would be to assess the wealth of a farmer, as there was no standard unit of value to make possible a comparison with other businesses. The growth of a monetary system made possible a means of comparison; but it took a very long time for a formal record-keeping system to become common. In 1494 an Italian mathematician, Luca Pacioli, wrote the first book describing a system of recording information that we now refer to as *double-entry book-keeping*.

Modern book-keeping systems are still based on the principles established in the fifteenth century, though they have been adapted to suit modern conditions. Double-entry book-keeping has proved the most convenient and effective way of recording information about a business, and even modern computerised recording systems are based on it.

In essence, Pacioli's recording system provides the answers to three basic questions that owners must ask:

- What profit has the business made?
- How much does the business owe?
- How much is owed to the business?

Record-keeping

For every business transaction there is a document that supports it. When you buy goods on credit, for example, you receive an *invoice* or bill from the suppliers. This gives the full details of the transaction—quantity, price, trade terms, etc.; and these details will be written into a record book called the *purchases day book*.

Over to you

What happens when we sell goods on credit, do you think?

The 60-second guide to ledger accounts, debits and credits ...

Once the details of transactions are safely recorded in the day books, the details are entered in or *posted to* the ledger accounts.

Ledger accounts work according to the double-entry system. This is based on the idea that each transaction has a double effect. A few examples should help to make this point clear.

1 If a business pays £5,000 in cash for a machine, the total value of the machinery the business owns will go up by £5,000 (in the machinery account), but its cash value will go down by £5,000 (in the cash account).

2 The business sold goods on credit to Tadhg Murphy for £4,000. Murphy now owes £4,000 to the business, and so he is called a *debtor* (the company is

owed a debt). The effect of this transaction is that the sales account goes up by £4,000, and we create a debtor's account in the name of Tadhg Murphy with £4,000.

3 Murphy decides to pay the business £1,000 to clear part of his debt, so the business's cash account will go up by £1,000, but the debtor account (Murphy) will go down by £1,000.

4 The business buys £3,000 worth of goods on credit from Teresa Ryan. The business now owes Ryan £3,000, and she is a **creditor** (the company owes) in the books of the business. The effect is that the purchases account increases by £3,000, and we create a creditor's account in the name of Teresa Ryan with £3,000.

5 The business now decides to pay Teresa Ryan £2,000 in cash. The amount it owes her (Teresa Ryan account) will go down by £2,000, but its bank account will also go down by £2,000.

You will see that all these transactions have a *dual* effect. This can involve both accounts going up, both going down, or one going up and the other going down. Nonetheless, there is always a *twofold effect* within the business. Double-entry book-keeping recognises this twofold effect of each transaction and is designed to record it.

But why record everything twice?

1 It provides valuable information about the effect of each transaction in respect of the business.

2 It provides a check on the accuracy of the recording system.

The account is the place where this twofold effect is recorded. An account either *receives* an amount or *gives* an amount. It is this receiving-and-giving effect that has given rise to two special terms commonly used in accountancy:

debit—meaning to receive, or value received

credit—meaning to give, or value given.

Accountants judge the twofold effect of all transactions from a receiving-and-giving point of view and therefore ask the following questions about every transaction:

1 Which account *receives* the amount—i.e. which account should be *debited*?
2 Which account *gives* this amount—i.e. which account should be *credited*?

In the following example you can see clearly that an account has two sides: a debit side and a credit side. Debits go on the left and credits on the right.

Take Note

Amount can be cash or goods

Recall transaction 1—what happened?

What did the business give? What did the business receive? It gave cash and it received a machine; therefore the two accounts affected are:

- the *machinery account*—the receiving account—which is debited.
- the *cash account*—the giving account—which is credited

When translated into accounting language—i.e. the company's accounts— it looks like this:

Machinery account

8 April	Cash	5,000

Cash account

8 April	Machinery	5,000

Over to you

Complete this procedure for transactions 2–5 (page 134).

What happens next? A flow chart to sum up

Documents received and sent—e.g. invoices, credit notes, debit notes, cheque stubs, cash receipts

↓

Day books—e.g. purchases day book, sales day book, cash books

↓

Ledger accounts

↓

Trial balance—a list of the balances in each of the individual ledger accounts

↓

Final accounts

The final analysis: the final accounts

At the end of the business trading year, the *trial balance* verifies that the double-entry rule was adhered to when the accounts were being written up. If the twofold effect of each transaction was recorded accurately, then the debits should equal the credits.

The trial balance with other information is used to prepare the *final accounts*. These final accounts will quickly give us the three basic pieces of information: the profit earned; the things we own (**assets**); and how much we owe (**liabilities**).

The four final accounts are:

- the trading account
- the profit and loss account
- the profit and loss appropriation account
- the balance sheet.

The trading account

The *trading account* is used to calculate total (but not final) profit. This profit is called gross profit, and it is the difference between what we sold the goods for and what it cost us to prepare them for sale, that is, the purchase price and other related costs. In essence, the trading account shows us the **gross profit**, which is simply

Sales – Cost of goods sold

Starship Enterprises Ltd
Trading account for the year ended 31 December 1999

Sales			170,000
Less sales returns			5,000
			165,000
Less cost of sales			
Opening stock (1 Jan. 1999)		12,000	
Purchases	116,000		
Less purchases returns	13,000	103,000	
Carriage inwards		1,500	
		116,500	
Less closing stock (31 Dec. 1999)		(11,500)	(105,000)
Gross profit			60,000

Over to you

1 What are the true (net) sales for the year for this business?

2 What is the cost of goods sold?

3 What is the gross profit for this trading period?

4 What is 'opening stock', and why is it included here?

5 What is 'closing stock', and why is it excluded? Consider: the closing stock of 1999 becomes the opening stock for 2000, and that stock will be sold during 2000.

6 Is the gross profit the pure profit the company can 'take home' at the end of a successful trading year?

Note

A business that manufactures goods must work out the total cost incurred in making the goods before it can calculate its gross profit. To do this, the first final account such a business must prepare is called the *manufacturing account*.

The profit and loss account

The end of the trading account becomes the opening of the **profit and loss account**; the gross profit is the opening item in this account. However, profit from trading is not the only source of income for a business. It has other ways of making money, such as interest earned from a deposit account, or rent received from property leased to tenants.

The business also has other expenses to cover (other than the cost of buying the goods), such as heat and light, insurance, and wages. These represent the *overheads* or expenses that are incurred in the day-to-day running of the business. The difference between the total income earned and the expenses incurred is the *net profit*. The trading, profit and loss account records only current income and expenditure. In essence, the profit and loss account is used to calculate:

> *Net profit = Total income – Total day-to-day expenses*

Starship Enterprises Ltd
Profit and loss account for the year ended 31 December 1999

Gross profit		60,000
Add other income:		
Rent received	6,000	
Interest received	400	6,400
		66,400
Less expenses:		
Advertising	1,200	
Lighting and heating	1,800	
Insurance	700	
Wages	25,100	
Rent and rates	2,000	
Telephone	1,600	
Repairs	250	
Bank charges	110	
Carriage outwards	200	32,960
Net profit		33,440

Over to you

1 What is the total income for this business this year?

2 What is the figure for expenses this year?

3 What is the true (net) profit of the business this year?

4 List any other expenses that a business might have.

5 Expenses can be classified as financial, administrative, and selling and distribution. Divide the expenses shown above into these categories.

6 If this company bought a new van, would it be entered under expenses in the profit and loss account? Why not?

The profit and loss appropriation account

Once the net profit has been ascertained, the company (or rather the board of directors) has to decide what to do with the funds. They have three choices:

- Retain them in the business, that is, **reinvest** or plough the profits back into the company.

- Distribute them among the shareholders as dividends.

- A mixture of these two options.

Net profit	33,440
Less dividend	(13,000)
Retained earnings	20,440

The balance sheet

The **balance sheet** is a financial 'snapshot' that captures a particular moment for a business. It is simply a list of what the business owns (assets) and what it owes (liabilities) on a particular date, usually the last day of the financial year. The assets and liabilities can be either short-term or long-term in nature.

Starship Enterprises Ltd
Balance Sheet as at 31 December 1999

Fixed assets:			
Premises			145,000
Vehicles			9,400
			154,400
Current assets:			
Stock	3,800		
Debtors	4,700		
Cash at bank	630		
Cash on hand	140	9,270	
Current liabilities:			
Creditors		(2,400)	6,870
Total net assets			161,270
Financed by:			
Share capital		100,000	
Reserves: profit and loss balance		20,440	
Long-term loan (debenture)		40,830	
Capital employed			161,270

working capital CA – CL

Over to you

1 If this business was to prepare a balance sheet on the following day, it might be different. Why?

2 Why are stock and debtors listed as current assets, while premises and equipment are listed as fixed assets?

Get the connection!

The accounts manager's survival guide

There are two simple rules: Record everything; and keep it simple.

Cash-based accounts

Because of the nature of the mini-enterprise and the life-span of the business, it is more convenient to trade in cash only. Selling goods on credit can cause problems.

Over to you

Can you foresee any problems that might arise? Use your initiative. If you think a sale might be lost because you have insisted on cash only—strictly no credit!—it might be advisable to take an executive decision; but make sure it is an informed one.

Records to keep

Keep a daily cash record. You need two record sheets: one for income and one for expenditure.

Do a monthly income and expenditure account. This will act as a self-checking system: the balance in the income and expenditure account should match the actual cash on hand or in the bank.

Take a look at the records kept by Home Bakers in their first month of trading.

Income record				
Date	Details	Total	Loans	Sales
1 Oct.	Loan from Allison's mother	10.00	10.00	
3 Oct.	Sold 20 scones	4.00		4.00
8 Oct.	Sold 30 scones	6.00		6.00
13 Oct.	Sold 40 scones	8.00		8.00
18 Oct.	Sold 45 scones	9.00		9.00
23 Oct.	Sold 50 scones	10.00		10.00
28 Oct.	Mid-term break	—	—	—
	Total	47.00	10.00	37.00

Expenditure record				
Date	Details	Total	Raw material	Labour	Other
2 Oct.	Ingredients	5.00	5.00		
3 Oct.	Labour	1.00		1.00	
	Packaging	2.00			2.00
	ESB	0.50			0.50
	Rent of kitchen	0.50			0.50

Date	Details	Total	Raw material	Labour	Other
8 Oct.	Labour	1.50		1.50	
	ESB	0.50			0.50
	Rent of kitchen	0.30			0.50
	Phone calls	1.00			1.00
	Stationery	3.00			3.00
13 Oct.	Labour	2.00		2.00	
	ESB	0.50			0.50
	Rent	0.50			0.50
18 Oct.	Labour	2.50		2.50	
	Ingredients	4.50	4.50		
	ESB	0.50			0.50
	Rent	0.50			0.50
	Packaging	2.50			2.50
23 Oct.	Labour	3.00		3.00	
	ESB	0.50			0.50
	Rent	0.50			0.50
	Paid Allison's mother	10.00			10.00
28	Mid-term break	—	—	—	—
	Total	43.00	9.50	10.00	23.50

Home Bakers
Income and expenditure account for the month
ended 31 October

Income:			
	Loan	10.00	
	Sales	37.00	47.00
Less expenses:			
	Raw material	9.50	
	Labour	10.00	
	Other	23.50	(43.00)
Excess income			4.00

In your mini-enterprise you can follow the example of Home Bakers in keeping track of your income and your expenditure.

CHAPTER TWENTY

No Man Is an Island

'Know your audience, know what you want to say, and try not to say too much.'

A story which highlights the importance of communication—it was claimed that before a battle, an officer sent a radio message: 'Send up reinforcements: we're going to advance.' The message was misheard and finally arrived as 'Send up three-and-fourpence: we're going to a dance.' It is one thing to communicate a message: it is quite a different thing to communicate that message effectively.

Businesses need to communicate with a large number of different groups of people and do so in a variety of ways. At one end of the scale there is the humble letter; at the other end there are the high-speed links between computers that pass millions of bits of information every minute.

Over to you

Can you identify the groups that businesses communicate with?

Get the message!

Many forms of communication are in use in the business world today, including written, visual, oral, electronic, etc.

Can you identify examples of each of these methods of communication?

Don't forget the non-verbal approach. 'Body language', and in particular facial expressions, can speak volumes.

Written communication

In any one day many methods of communication can be used to get the message across. Some of the most common forms of written communication are letters, memos, reports, and minutes.

Letters

Businesses write letters for many reasons, including contacting customers and suppliers. Business letters often contain important and complex information, which must be given clearly and accurately. Depending on how well it is prepared, a business letter can enhance or tarnish a firm's reputation with the recipient.

Sample business letter

Here is a letter sent by a company to a potential customer:

TALLAGHT RECORDS LTD
Oldbawn Road · Dublin 24

Mr Seán Joyce   14 February 1999
Rathcormack Road
Fermoy
Co. Cork   Our ref. AR98/3

Dear Mr Joyce,

Thank you for your letter of 27 January and for the demonstration tape enclosed with it.

I am afraid that our company does not normally produce music of the kind performed by you on the tape, specialising as we do in traditional Irish music. Even if we were to change our policy, we do not think that the routine on your demonstration tape would complement our existing catalogue or appeal to our audience.

With regret, therefore, I am returning your tape with this letter. I hope you succeed in finding a suitable producer for your music.

Yours sincerely,

Martin Flanagan

Martin Flanagan,
Managing Director

Enc.

Memos

When you are communicating with people *within* your own company, a less formal approach is adopted.

Most of the written communication within a business is in the form of *memorandums*—'memos' for short. A memo is an informal type of letter, which should be kept short and to the point. Though they are less formal than letters, it must be remembered that memos are part of the official communications of the business and should be treated seriously.

Memorandum

To: Anne Clarke
From: Martin Flanagan
Subject: Letters from Seán Joyce
Date: 14 Feb. 1998

I have received yet another demo tape from Seán Joyce, Fermoy. This makes a total of four received in the last two years.

I have pointed out to him that the kind of music he performs would not be published by us—and, frankly, is not likely to be published by anyone.

In future, would you please reply to any further applications from him, referring to our past correspondence and asking him not to send us any more tapes.

Reports

A report is a detailed written document on a particular subject, generally used where a longer message has to be communicated within the company, or by an outside firm working for the business as contractors or consultants. It can be compiled by an individual or by a group and usually contains standard sections, though the structure and headings can differ greatly.

A typical report would include:

- *terms of reference:* the objectives of the report
- *findings*: the results of the investigation carried out
- a *conclusion:* this will usually also contain recommendations about the subject of the report.

Visual communication

Another important means of communicating your message is the use of visual aids. Visual aids make communication more interesting and serve to emphasise and clarify important aspects of the information being delivered. It has also been proved that information people have *seen* remains with them longer.

Over to you

Visual aids are employed by many businesses to get their message across. Can you name some?

Electronic communication

Increasingly, businesses are using electronic forms of communication, including *fax*, *videoconferencing*, and *e-mail*.

Oral communication

Despite the increasing use of new forms of communication, the individual voice still remains effective. Oral communication includes telephone conversations, meetings, interviews, and casual conversations. In oral communication it is important to get the message right first time, and this usually requires some preparation, particularly in the planning of a meeting. Business meetings range from a few people getting together informally in an office to a full annual general meeting (AGM) with a set agenda, to which everyone concerned with the company is invited.

Assignment

You and your friends have decided to plan a holiday together, and you have volunteered to make the arrangements. You have spoken on the phone to a company that runs camping holidays in Dingle. Here are your notes from the phone conversation:

Skellig Camp, PO Box 24, Dingle, Co. Kerry
Ready-erected tents or empty plots for own tents on west side of camp
Some vacancies in August
Cost: £100 per week + £5 per person for erected tent
Site only: £20
Gas cylinders: £5
Sleeping-bag hire: £5 per person per week (or take own)

They can arrange food hamper for arrival (also one for vegetarians)—£5 per person

Write a letter to the company, booking two weeks in the middle of August for eight people. You will be taking one four-person tent with you, and you all have your own sleeping-bags. You would like one gas cylinder, and a food hamper for eight people, two of whom are vegetarians.

Don't forget to work out the total cost, and to send a 10 per cent deposit.

Organising a meeting

Two people are closely involved in the preparations for the AGM: the chairperson and the company secretary. They come together to plan the meeting, as it is important that all meetings are structured in an appropriate, clear and orderly way.

Before the meeting, a notice is sent out to those who will be attending, giving details of the time, place, and agenda. The *agenda* is a list of the items to be considered at the meeting.

Notice

The annual general meeting of Tallaght Records Ltd will be held on Monday 22 April in the Oldbawn Hotel, Tallaght, at 10:15 a.m.

Agenda

1. Apologies
2. Minutes
3. Matters arising from minutes
4. Correspondence
5. Directors' report of company performance this year
6. Presentation of final accounts
7. Election of directors
8. Special matters: discussion of proposed take-over bid
9. Any other business

The meeting will be followed by lunch in the grill room at 12:45 p.m.

Martin Flanagan   Anne Clarke
Chairperson   Company Secretary

Play by the rules: running the meeting

The *chairperson* of the meeting makes sure the meeting runs smoothly. This is often the managing director of the company. The chairperson acts like a referee, making sure the agenda is followed and that opinions get a fair hearing, and strives to be impartial and to facilitate the meeting rather than dominating the proceedings.

A case in point

Martin Flanagan has recently been appointed managing director and is preparing to chair his first AGM. While he has attended many meetings in the past, he has never chaired one before, and he has asked the company secretary to draw up a memo summarising the chairperson's duties.

Memorandum

To: Martin Flanagan
From: Anne Clarke
Subject: Chairing next month's AGM
Date: 25 March 1999

I have drawn up a list of the duties performed by the chairperson, as requested.

1.   Open the meeting, and make sure the minimum number of people (a 'quorum') is present so that the meeting can officially begin.

2.   Follow the agenda, and make sure each topic is discussed.

3.   Keep order, remain impartial, and allow each participant to have their say.

4.   Put motions to a vote, and declare the result. Traditionally, the chairperson does not take part in the voting but will cast a vote to break a deadlock. This will usually be a vote for the 'status quo', i.e. against a proposed change of policy.

5.   As secretary to the meeting, I will notify the participants of the agenda in advance. At the beginning of the meeting I will read out the minutes of the previous AGM (which I sent you yesterday), and during the meeting I will take notes of matters discussed and of decisions made. After the meeting I will use these notes when writing the minutes for the next meeting.

After the meeting …

Following the meeting, the secretary will write and circulate the **minutes** of the meeting. These are not a word-for-word account of everything that was said (that would be a **transcript**) but an account of the main matters that were covered, together with details of the decisions that were taken and of those responsible for implementing each of the decisions.

Get the connection!

1 In your mini-enterprise you may have reason to contact your customers, suppliers or work-mates in writing. Suppose a supplier has contacted you in writing about a new raw material that could be more effective but is also more costly: when replying, which will you use, a letter or a memo? Why?

2 Never under-estimate the power of the visual. Packaging or advertising material could send your sales volume soaring.

3 The internet, especially the worldwide web, could prove an untapped resource for your business.

4 Word of mouth can be extremely beneficial to your business, or absolutely detrimental. It is important to remember that when customers have a problem they will often talk among themselves rather than ask the provider to remedy the problem.

5 Keeping your own house in order can be achieved by keeping the channels of communication open at all times. Many internal communication problems can be resolved if they are discussed at the early stages. Open and frank communication is the solution, not sweeping it under the carpet.

6 Depending on the size of your mini-enterprise, board meetings can be either formal or fairly informal. Approaching meetings in a structured way will allow business to be dealt with quickly and efficiently. The following structure could be used when holding your meetings, whether daily or monthly (depending on your circumstances).

Sample agenda

Mini-enterprise board meeting

1. Introduction, and attendance taken
2. Minutes of last meeting
3. Production report
4. Sales report
5. Finance report
6. General manager's comments
7. Any other business (future events; plan for week)

---

7 Some mini-enterprises may hold an AGM, which is open to all shareholders of the business and is normally held at the end of the term or school year. The directors present a report on the year's activities, and the shareholders can voice opinions about the conduct of the business.

The records or minutes of the weekly board meetings will form the backbone of the annual report. If the company plans to continue its existence into the following year, the new directors are elected at the AGM.

8 Preparations for the AGM:

Check-list:

- date, time, and place
- Draw up the notice and agenda, and send it to each shareholder.
- Each director or manager must draw up a summary report of the events and activities in their department.
- Speeches: preparation is the key. Follow Mark Twain's example: 'It takes me at least three weeks to prepare a good impromptu speech'.
- Refreshments

Remember

It might be a good idea to acknowledge the people who helped you by sending them a *thank-you note*.

CHAPTER TWENTY-ONE

Where To from Here

Whether a business is a success or a failure, it is sometimes a good idea for the business to stop and assess itself; it will help to see where the business is, and perhaps help it find its path for the future.

One method of doing this is to perform a 'SWOT' analysis. This involves a business examining its *strengths, weaknesses, opportunities,* and *threats.* It gives the business an opportunity to focus on the main issues, and aids effective decision-making.

Over to you

Can you identify the possible strengths, weaknesses, opportunities and threats an enterprise might experience?

A business cannot stand still. If it doesn't grow, then it declines. There are several paths to growth:

1 **Using the existing product**, explore new market segments.
2 **Add new features** to attract new customers and possibly increase sales and profits.
3 **A private limited company** may decide to go public and gain a Stock Exchange quotation.

Distinguish between a private limited company and a public limited company. In your opinion, why would a private company go public?

4 **Expand into foreign markets.** As Ireland is a member of the European Union, this option is relatively straightforward.

What are the advantages of exporting? Can you foresee any problems a potential exporter might encounter?

5 Hedging your bets. Diversify into new products—related or unrelated. This might entail developing a range of products so that the business can gain maximum use of the various stages of the product's life-cycle.

Over to you
How can a business use the product's life-cycle to maximum effect?

6 Don't keep all your eggs in one basket. Get involved in other businesses (*related* or *unrelated diversification*). Related diversification means developing into other businesses but within the same industry: for example, Proctor and Gamble are involved in many businesses—detergents, toothpaste, cosmetics, and nappies; though these businesses appear very different they are within the same industry, the consumer goods industry.

An enterprise can engage in related diversification by becoming involved in the following activities:

Related diversification

- **backward integration**—becoming involved in a business at an earlier stage in the chain of production: for example, a chocolate manufacturer buying a cocoa plantation

Backward

- **forward integration**—becoming involved in a business at a later stage in the production chain: for example, breweries in England buying pubs

Forward

Horizontal

- **horizontal integration**—becoming involved in businesses that are in competition with your existing business or a business that produces complementary products: for example, a car manufacturer buying into the tyre industry.

Unrelated diversification means engaging in activities that have no connection with the existing activities of the business.

If a business pursues the path of diversification (into different products or businesses) and thus creates a business portfolio, it would be no harm for the enterprise to take time off to undertake a portfolio analysis. Like a SWOT analysis, this will help the business to focus on its activities. This involves identifying the main products or businesses making up the enterprise. These are called *strategic business units* (SBUs).

The next step involves analysing each SBU and assessing its attractiveness and the strength of its position in the market or industry. A well-known method used for carrying out this procedure is the BCG (Boston Consulting Group) growth-share matrix. BCG has identified four categories into which the various products and businesses of an enterprise may fall.

Relative market share

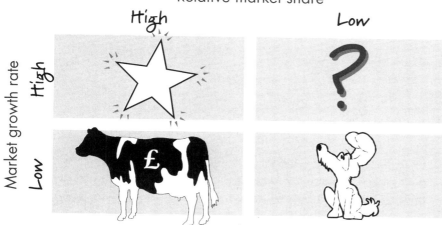

High growth, high market share

Heavy investment is often needed to finance the rapid growth. Eventually growth will slow down, and the star should convert into a cash cow.

Low growth, high market share

Little investment is needed, as these products or businesses are established and successful. The cash milked from the cow can be used to develop other areas of the business.

High growth, low market share

Money needs to be invested to retain the market share. The enterprise must decide which sections (SBUs) to develop or drop.

Low growth, low market share

This section is probably in decline, and there is no promise of a large intake of cash.

Performing this analysis allows an enterprise to make decisions: which promising question marks to make into stars so that they will become cash cows as the market matures. Decisive action needs to be taken regarding dogs, and some question marks, to avoid throwing good money after bad.

7 A merger. This is when two or more businesses combine: for example, Avonmore PLC and Waterford PLC.

Over to you
What is the name of this merged company?

Take Note

Is your product/
service:
a star
a cash cow
a question mark
a dog?

8 **A take-over.** This is when one business buys another: for example, when Tesco bought out the Quinnsworth chain, or Statoil took over Jet. A take-over is not as easy as it seems, as the Competition Authority, a state agency, will only sanction take-overs that are deemed not to be 'anti-competitive'.

Over to you

Why are take-overs monitored by the Competition Authority?

9 **Forming a strategic alliance or a joint venture.** Two businesses co-operate on a project or business venture; they pool their skills and resources but remain separate. Ford and Mazda formed a strategic alliance that proved mutually beneficial.

10 **Becoming a franchisor.** If you wish to expand your successful enterprise but don't wish to be directly involved in the expansion, you can sell your idea, name or product to somebody else. They pay you a fee and a percentage of their profits. The franchisee runs the business in an identical fashion to the original one—copied and equalled. In essence, the original business is a tried and tested formula, which should guarantee success if the blueprint is followed exactly.

Go to Chapter 12

1 What advantages are there from the point of view (a) of the franchisor and (b) of the franchisee in this form of business?

2 Give examples of franshises operating in Ireland.

3 Can you envisage any problems that each party might encounter?

4 Can you identify the reasons why a business is expanded?

5 What are the factors that affect the expansion route chosen?

Enough is enough: when to call a halt!

Sometimes if the business isn't running smoothly and is making a loss or having cash flow problems, it might be time to move on. Perhaps the business can be sold and the proceeds used for a fresh start.

Can you think of five reasons why a business might not be a success?

Get the connection!

1 Once your business is operating, it is important to monitor its progress by keeping tabs on sales, profit, and the ability to pay debts as they arise.

2 It may be necessary to adapt or alter the product or service to meet customers' needs and to expand sales.

3 Try to broaden your horizons. If you can find a market beyond the obvious customers, you may not need that summer job, and it may pave the way for self-employment.

4 Some mini-enterprises may have to *liquidate* or wind up operations before the end of the school year. It's important to handle the closing-down process correctly.

- Have an end-of-term sale to sell off any remaining stock.
- If you have any unused stocks of raw materials, try to sell them off also.
- Make sure all your customers have paid you—and that you have paid all your suppliers.
- Once all outstanding bills have been paid, what's left is profit.
- If you have shareholders, you have a responsibility to let them know how their investment performed.
    1. Hold an AGM.
    2. Distribute your profits.
    3. Return the original capital investment to your shareholders.

Note

The shareholder should have proof of their shareholding (a share certificate) to claim their entitlement to their capital investment. Rigid rules would suggest 'no certificate, no money'; however, it is good business practice to keep a record of the shareholders and the value of their shareholding and to return the investment, together with any dividend, to the shareholder whether they can produce a certificate or not. It is not only good business practice: it could also be considered common courtesy.

And finally ...

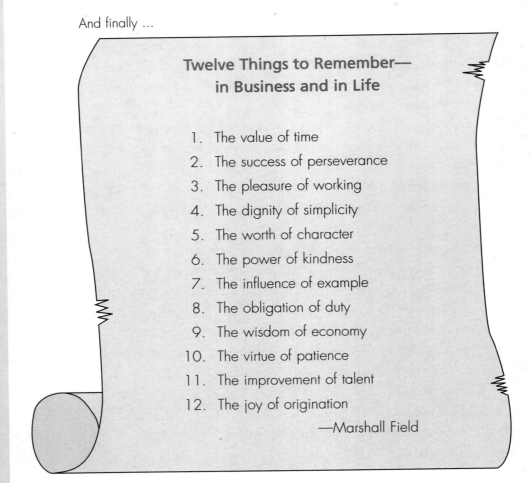

**Twelve Things to Remember—
in Business and in Life**

1. The value of time
2. The success of perseverance
3. The pleasure of working
4. The dignity of simplicity
5. The worth of character
6. The power of kindness
7. The influence of example
8. The obligation of duty
9. The wisdom of economy
10. The virtue of patience
11. The improvement of talent
12. The joy of origination

—Marshall Field

The last word goes to Charles Handy:

'Money-making is a means to a life, not the point of it.'